Celebrating The Wedding
of Policy and Economics

A History of
The Frank E. Seidman
Distinguished Award
in Political Economy

with highlights of
acceptance papers by
fifteen eminent
award recipients.

by Mel G. Grinspan

Published by Rhodes College
Memphis, Tennessee

Copyright © Rhodes College, Memphis, Tennessee, 1989

Library of Congress Cataloging-in-Publication Data
Grinspan, Mel G.
   Celebrating the wedding of policy and economics.
   "Including highlights of acceptance papers written by fifteen eminent economists
   who received the award."
1. Seidman Distinguished Award in Political Economy. 2. Economic policy. I. Title.
HD75.G75 1989   338.9   89-10270

ACKNOWLEDGEMENTS

The Award By-laws specify that a member of the Seidman family be a member of its Board of Trustees. P. K. Seidman, now Emeritus, served originally as its chair. He was followed by Lawrence J. Seidman, who now is chair and serves the Award admirably and effectively. His advice and counsel in directing the activities of the Award are deeply appreciated.

For their help in producing this volume, I also give special thanks to Gail Stroud and Loyd Templeton.

TO P. K. SEIDMAN

Whose foresight, insight, perseverance, strength and resources have made this memorial to his brother what it is today: an internationally recognized award which has earned the respect of eminent economists all over the world.

CONTENTS

PREFACE

The Frank E. Seidman distinguished Award In Political Economy was established in memory of Frank E. Seidman by Mr. and Mrs. P. K. Seidman. The host college for the Award is Rhodes College, a liberal arts college established in 1848 and located in Memphis, Tennessee. An honorarium of $15,000 is given to the recipient of the Award.

In the sixteen years of its existence, it has earned an enviable international reputation in an area of economics whose definition is still subject to debate by economists and social scientists all over the world. That the term "political economy" should embrace the interdisciplinary partnership of economics and the other social sciences on a "real-life" basis appears to be an accepted thesis by a growing number of economists and political scientists. Some envision the emergence of a new "socioeconomics," a discipline which more clearly embodies the wedding of policy and economics.

This history of the Award, especially the highlights of their acceptance papers, becomes somewhat of a commentary on the changing conditions of the economy from 1974 to 1989 as discussed by the fifteen recipients, world-reknown economists who relate their views of those conditions to the works which made them famous. Also included are observations of other equally respected economists who presented the Awards to the recipients.

A few words regarding the highlights of the recipients' acceptance papers: though we would have preferred to do so, it was not feasible to reprint the papers in their entirety. In presenting the highlights of each, it was my intention to give the reader only a cursory exposure to the author's thoughts.

There must have been a certain prescience guiding the first recipient, Gunnar Karl Myrdal, who wrote his acceptance paper on "What is Political Economy?" It is a question that has been discussed and debated rigorously by those associated with the Award throughout its sixteen year history. Many of the concepts are included in this volume. They are, in some minds, a bold reflection of the zeitgeist of contemporary economic thought.

Mel. G. Grinspan
Director of the Award

•ONE•

The First Three Years

The economy of the United States was entering a state of trauma in the latter months of 1973. The Organization of Petroleum Exporting Countries (OPEC) had instituted price increases on its oil, boosting the cost of a barrel of the precious commodity from $2.50 to $10.00, which in turn, caused shockwaves that jolted already-rising inflation to new heights, elevated unemployment to new post World War II levels, drove trade balances into hitherto unknown thresholds, and phased in Phase IV of President Richard Nixon's wage and price controls which were vexing American business. To capsulize what was happening to people and their pocketbooks during these convulsive times, the sages introduced a new criterion by which to judge the human condition. It was called the Misery Index (the total of the percentage of inflation and unemployment) and it hovered restlessly at a high 15% by the end of 1973.

The twists and turns of economic actions and reactions resulting from these events were also causing misery to many economists who found it prudent to restudy the principles on which their theories were based. The vessels, which had safely contained heretofore acceptable, though arguable, economic interpretations, were leaking. Orthodox explanations for such ailments as a feverish inflation were highly suspect. (A number of diverse opinions on inflation are discussed by many of the Award's recipients in another section). Regardless of what one's economic arguments were, they didn't seem to hold water.

It was during this unsettled time (but not because of it) that Mr. P. K. and Mrs. Leone Seidman, he a partner in the international accounting firm of Seidman & Seidman (now BDO/Seidman), decided to memorialize his brother and fellow partner, Frank E. Seidman, who had died the year before. Because of Frank E.'s abiding interest in the subject as a columnist, lecturer and political adviser, P. K. and Leone concluded that awarding achievement in political economy would be the appropriate manner to honor his brother's memory. It was also a fitting time for such recognition because the human condition was receiving a goodly share of scrutiny by the commonly accepted components of political economy, policy and economic theory.

There were other stars in P. K.'s eyes as the idea took form. He had lived in Memphis, Tennessee since 1933 when he arrived from Grand Rapids, Michigan, to open an office for the accounting firm. In the ensuing years, he became one of the city's staunchest supporters and most solid citizens. He foresaw in the Award not only an appropriate tribute to his brother, but also an opportunity to bring, as a supplementary goal, international notice to his adopted home and first-hand exposure of its citizens to a vitally important subject and its proponents. That he succeeded in reaching that supplementary goal is attested to by the remarks made by James Tobin, 1981 Nobel Laureate in Economics, when he presented the Award to Robert Triffin in Memphis, in 1988. Dr. Tobin said, "Robert, let me introduce you to this audience. Memphis is a long way from Brussels, not even that close to Washington, New York, New Haven or Boston. But as you and Lois (Mrs. Triffin) are finding out, your new friends here are not only extremely hospitable, but also deeply interested in political economy and political economists, among whom their tastes are sophisticated and discriminating."

Another significant aspect of the program was to be its administration by a Memphis educational institution. Memphis State University (MSU) was chosen for this role. An important part of the Tennessee higher education system, MSU was emerging as a major southern university. It welcomed the opportunity to affiliate itself with the Award and the benefits the Award promised. The MSU Foundation became the Award's sponsor on December 27, 1973, with the signing of an agreement between P. K. and Leone Seidman and the foundation.

The arrangement called for the establishment of an Award Board of Trustees which would "provide the overall guidance and control of the annual Award." The Board was also to be responsible for the operation of the Selection Committee and "shall have complete jurisdiction over the implementation of the criteria in accord with the stated objectives of the Award." Though since revised, the original objective was "to recognize and encourage economists who are attempting to extend their methodology into the interdependent areas of the other social sciences." (Present objectives and criteria will be found elsewhere in this volume.) The Trustees were also to have final approval, though not the actual selection, of the recipient nominated by the Selection committee.

The Award's original agreement also specified the makeup of the Board. It was to be as follows (those named to the first Board are also shown):

POSITION	TERM OF INDIVIDUAL
Representative of Seidman Family *P. K. Seidman*	Indefinite
President of MSU *Billy M. Jones*	Indefinite
Chairman of Department of Eco- nomics, MSU *Kurt Flexner*	Indefinite
Resident of Memphis, Tennessee area *Abe Plough*	2 years
Resident of Grand Rapids, Michigan area *Richard Gillett*	2 years
President or Member of Executive Committee, American Economic Association *Walter W. Heller*	2 years
Past or Present Member of the Presi- dent's Council of Economic Advisers *Paul W. McCracken*	1 year
Director *Arthur A. Bayer*	At the will of the Board

Memphis, Tennessee and Grand Rapids, Michigan were especially earmarked for Board representation, the former because of the desire to tie-in the Memphis business community with the Award; Grand Rapids, because Frank E. Seidman had lived the greater part of his life there first in government and later when he opened a branch office of Seidman & Seidman and became a prominent civic leader in the area. The Memphis businessman chosen was the late Abe Plough, Chairman of the Board, Plough Inc., one of the world's important cosmetic and proprietary medicine manufacturers. The Grand Rapids businessman was Richard Gillett, Chairman of the Board of Old Kent Bank and Trust, one of Michigan's largest banks. Mr. Gillett, now retired, continues to serve on the Award Board.

Other representation on the Board was pinpointed to assure proper participation by the sponsoring university and by acknowledged leaders in the economics profession.

The original agreement also noted that the P. K. and Leone Seidman Foundation had given to the Memphis State University Foundation $101,322.38 in marketable securities with the income from the securities applied toward the annual expense budget of the Award, less its share of the expenses of the budget of the Foundation. The endowment was increased to $150,000 several months later. Currently, the fund approximates $500,000.

So the die had been cast. The Award was a reality.

The news of the creation of the Award and the selection of Memphis State University was hailed as an important step in gaining recognition for the city of Memphis and for the university. Editorial comment in the Memphis papers was enthusiastic. *The Commercial Appeal* asserted, "The establishment of the Award will make Memphis and Memphis State University the seat of one of the most prestigious honors in the world." *The Memphis Press Scimitar* described the Award as a "plus for MSU."

With the initial glow of the announcement surrounding it, the small group responsible for pounding out the Award details began its implementation.

Prior to the signing of the agreement, P. K. had been consulting with Drs. Arthur Bayer and Kurt Flexner of the Memphis State Department of Economics, on the philosophical underpinnings of the Award, its criteria and objectives. It was from these sessions that the heart and soul of the Award were styled and flesh put on the skeleton of the idea.

As might be expected, the consultants had long and rigorous discussions on what constituted political economy, and who were the political economists. Agreement on these items was essential in order to arrive at workable objectives of the Award and criteria by which recipients would be selected.

The very nature of such discussions contained the seeds of arguments which have been nurtured each time the Selection Committees and the Boards of Trustees have met since the Award's inception. It is a tribute to the original group as well as to the various Boards and Selection Committees that followed, that the rational process has prevailed and consensus reached. Eventually the participants always agree on guidelines by which to interpret the criteria and reach a decision on whom the recipient should be. But inevitably the debate is revived as each new Selection Committee meets to discuss its responsibility. The very essence of what constitutes political economy seems to be so ephemeral and controversial that the most astute minds in the economic discipline find it difficult to reach agreement. There are strong opinions on the issue and only rarely are they *not* aired.

That the Award and its criteria are a vibrant, living entity is shown by these on-going discussions–debates would better describe the exercises–and by the fact that at least temporary agreement is attained on how the criteria should be altered to help future Committees and Boards reach future consensus: the key word, though, is "temporary" because in its sixteen-year history, those criteria have been revised four times.

Arthur Bayer, first Award Director, former Dean of Undergraduate Studies at Babson College and now Professor of Economics at that institution, summed up the work of the Selection Committees well during his presentation of the 1982 Award to Janos Kornai. Bayer said, "...one is struck by the unselfish dedication and encouragement given by all associated with this laudable endeavor. Economists who certainly have many other professional obligations have graciously given of their time to hammer out in annual sessions even more objective and meaningful interpretations of the Award procedures and standards."

It was the first Board meeting held in Memphis, Tennessee, February 28, 1974, that the first set of objectives and criteria, after much scrutiny and discussion, finally were adopted. It was also decided that the Award should be given in the ambience of a formal banquet in Memphis.

To assure an even greater involvement of the Memphis community, it was decided to invite the Economic Club of Memphis (also founded by P. K. Seidman) to co-host the annual banquets with MSU and the Award. This group of prominent business, academic and professional people proved to be an excellent partner not only because of its inherent interest in the subject but also because of its enthusiastic support.

The Board then climaxed its first meeting by choosing as its first recipient Gunnar Karl Myrdal of Sweden who would receive the Award on May 29, 1974. P. K. was designated to travel to Santa Barbara, California, to notify Dr. Myrdal, then a Fellow at the Robert Maynard Hutchins Center for the Study of Democratic Institutions.

The naming of Myrdal stirred up some heated discussion especially in the South. It appeared to many as an aggressively uninhibited way to introduce the Award. Some took exception to his liberal views, those opinions being exacerbated by his adverse assertions on life in the south. He was best known in that region for his book published in 1944, *An American Dilemma: The Negro Problem and American Democracy.* The book was cited in the 1954 U.S. Supreme Court decision on school desegregation.

When he returned in 1974 to accept the Award, Myrdal said, "This is only the second time I've been in the Deep South in more than 30 years. At the time we were here first, it was dirt roads. Your political and economic life was determined by where you kept the Negro. What has happened with desegregation has been a tremendous liberation."

Thomas BeVier, in *The Commercial Appeal*, March 27, 1974, in an article headed "Myrdal Returns to Memphis", wrote, "Looking back through 'Dilemma,' we realized we had been at fault in assuming Myrdal was like some sort of criminal returning to the scene of his crime. Despite its harsh criticism, the work centers on something Myrdal calls the American Creed, the belief that the average American embraces the ideal of equal opportunity and justice for all regardless of the narrowness and bigotry he sometimes displays. Myrdal all but said that the changes in race relations we have seen in the last quarter century would occur. Taken from the perspective of 1944, it is likely the Swedish scholar had more faith in us than we had in ourselves."

In the wake of national and international commentary, pro and con, Myrdal received the first Award, and so the program was launched. Noteworthy is the fact that a short-time later Myrdal was named co-Nobel Laureate in Economics with Frederick Hayek.

The selection of John Kenneth Galbraith in 1975 also met with some controversy. As a widely-known author, former Ambassador to India, Economics Professor at Harvard, and one closely associated with liberal Democratic politics, he had a high public profile which was not shared by some of the other recipients who followed him. There were some detractors who referred to him as one who was too closely biased by Socialistic sentiment. Yet his pronouncements bespoke moderation. Galbraith said he rejoiced in being called a political economist. In an interview in *The Commercial Appeal* May 31, 1975, he said, "In modern times, power, the surrogate word for politics, has become increasingly a force in economic life...The modern corporation, the modern trade unions are instruments for the exercise of economic power...Economics has been excluding these powers from its attention."

The third year of the Award witnessed the choice of Kenneth E. Boulding as recipient, a swing to a moderate after two liberals. But another swing was in store for the Award. It took place in 1976.

•TWO•

The Move to Rhodes

What began as a mutually beneficial relationship between the Award and Memphis State University came to an abrupt end. On June 22, 1976, midst disagreement on what prompted the action, MSU announced that it had cancelled its participation in the Award "citing expense as the major factor for the university's withdrawal." (*The Memphis Press-Scimitar*, June 22, 1976).

The same news article continued, "However, P. K. Seidman, senior consultant in the international accounting firm of Seidman & Seidman, said MSU gave up its joint sponsorship of the program because it had received 'some flack' about the liberal recipients of the Awards." P. K. then added that he was seeking sponsorship by some other educational institution. Meantime, Dr. Billy Mac Jones, president of MSU, denied that criticism of the Award recipients played any part in the university's decision. He emphasized that the decision had nothing to do with academic freedom and that the decision was based on the availability of funds to be used for such programs as the Award. The availability of funds took on another dimension when there arose a disagreement on the transfer of the Award Endowment to the successor sponsoring educational institution. This matter was settled in Chancery Court to the satisfaction of the charitable trust funding the Award.

The announcement stirred up additional comments in an editorial dated June 27, 1976, in *The Commercial Appeal*. In alluding to the first three recipients, Myrdal, Galbraith and Boulding, the editorial said, "All of them have written and said things that some people don't like to hear. The field of economics is composed of people of very different and opposing views. In an extremely inexact science, all the experts have been wrong sometimes. Those who have dared to argue for new points of view often have found themselves unpopular. But in presenting something like the Seidman Award, there should be no bias...we need thinkers and thought provokers. An independent spirit is to be admired in making an economics award, especially when it is done under the aegis of a university where the unrestrained quest for knowledge is fundamental. And it's important that this spirit be nurtured in Memphis and that the Seidman Award be comfortably based here."

P. K. strongly agreed that the Award should be based in Memphis and felt that Southwestern at Memphis (now Rhodes College) was the logical institution to become the new sponsor.

Southwestern at Memphis, which changed its name to Rhodes in 1984 to honor a former president, had its roots in Clarksville, Tennessee. It underwent several name changes while there, became affiliated with the Presbyterian Church in 1873, was reorganized after the Reconstruction Era and moved to Memphis in 1925. Its name was changed to Southwestern at Memphis and then, in 1984, to Rhodes College, in honor of Dr. Peyton Nalle Rhodes who served as President and in other capacities from 1926 until his death in 1984. Rhodes is currently recognized as one of the most highly respected liberal arts colleges in the country.

Dr. James H. Daughdrill, Jr., President of Rhodes College and P. K. Seidman began discussions shortly after MSU withdrew its administrative support from the Award. About six weeks later on August 16, 1976, the two announced agreement on Rhodes College assuming the sponsorship of the Award. P. K. said, "Southwestern (now Rhodes) was the only choice as host campus. With its reputation for excellence and stability, it was a natural choice, I wanted the Award to stay in Memphis."

Dr. Daughdrill said that the college's great interest in the Award was based on its desire "to expand the intellectual stimulation of our academic program by having world-renowned political economists visit the college and Memphis." He also suggested that, though the college would incur some expense in assuming sponsorship, "it is very small in comparison to the importance of recognition the Award makes."

In agreeing to the sponsoring of the Award, the Rhodes Board of Trustees set forth four guiding principles dealing with (1) academic freedom and censorship: (2) the college's role as a product of the free-enterprise system, (3) its pursuit of knowledge, and the following statement as the last of the four principles: "The principle of intellectual integrity requires that the Award not be based on doctrinaire political or economic views, but that selection of nominees be considered from the full spectrum of political economists, whether American or non-American; and without regard to race, color or religious affiliation."

With the move to the new host college, it was also necessary to name a new Award Director. Chosen for that position was Mel G. Grinspan, who also played an active role in bringing the

Award to Southwestern at Memphis. He was Distinguished Service Professor in the Department of Business Administration and a former chief executive officer of a prominent southern chain of department stores.

THREE

Selection Procedure:

The Washington Connection

Beginning in 1976, the practice of convening the Selection Committee and the Board of Trustees in Washington
was instituted. It was felt that location was more accessible to
the people involved and that having a one-day meeting to conduct the Award's business in the nation's capital would add prestige to the Award. Since then, the meetings have evolved into
two-day sessions with the Selection Committee meeting on a
Thursday afternoon and the Board meeting on Friday morning
to consider the Committees recommendations and to conduct
other Award business.

These sessions in Washington are not without lighter, more
social hours. An activity which has become traditional is the
Thursday evening dinner to which past and present members of
the Committee, the Board and their spouses are invited. The
after-dinner, free-for-all conversation usually centers on an off-
the-record intellectual repast on current economic conditions,
what caused them and where they will lead. From the liberal
explanations of Leon Keyserling, the Chairman of the first President's Council of Economic Advisers under President Harry

14

Truman, to the mild-mannered but clear conservatism of Arthur Burns, the dinner guests have always been treated to provocative, stimulating opinions on what's wrong or what's right with our economic health (or lack thereof).

What is not discussed or made known is the Selection committee's recommendation, the result of its meeting earlier that day.

The Award By-Laws state that the Selection Committee is to submit a slate of three candidates to the Board in order of the Committee's preference. The process by which the Committee reaches that point is the culmination of a rather complex procedure.

In the fall of each year, approximately 1200 economists all over the world, predominantly in academia but including those in the private sector, are sent explanatory material and requests to submit nominations for the following year's Award. Since this process began, an average of 110 economists have been nominated annually by 235 nominators from 30 states and 11 foreign countries. In those nominations, approximately 120 American and foreign educational institutions are represented as well as 20 corporate and economics-oriented associations.

This information is summarized and integrated into a booklet which includes biographical and other pertinent data on those receiving the most ballots and is sent to the Selection Committee for its perusal six weeks prior to its meeting in Washington. It is at the Committee's meeting in Washington that the Selection process reaches its peak. After considering all nominees, the Committee studiously and painstakingly reduces the list to a smaller number of nominees, whose qualifications are discussed in detail. Their contributions to political economics, their fit with the interdisciplinary Award criteria, their comparison to others in the group in terms of past, present and future significance to the profession–all these factors are thoroughly aired until, by whatever number of secret ballots and further discussions are necessary, the Committee is able to agree on three candidates whose names are presented, in order of preference, to the Board the following morning by the Chairman of the Committee

The three candidates' credentials having been presented in detail, the Board then engages in its own discussion and finally agrees on the recipient. From a procedural standpoint, the Award By-laws specify that if the Board does not accept any of the Committee's recommendations, the matter is then returned to the Committee for another choice which is again presented to the Board for its decision.

As mentioned before, an integral part of each meeting is the discussion devoted to improving the selection process, the primary objective being the refining of a procedure which represents the highest levels of interdisciplinary professionalism, objectivity and integrity.

After the Board makes its decision, the recipient is informed of his/her selection and the planning for the Award presentation begins. The recipient is required to attend the formal Award banquet, to address the approximate 250 Memphis business, professional and academic leaders, to meet with a group of Rhodes College students, and to write an acceptance paper which is published and circulated to libraries all over the United States as well as to selected economists throughout the world. Highlights of the recipient's papers appear elsewhere in this volume.

The $15,000 honorarium is thought to be the second largest monetary award for recognition in economics, the first being the Nobel Prize. Discussion on increasing it from its original tax-free $10,000 to its present $15,000 began in 1981. Members of the Board, in discussing ways and means to broaden recognition of the Award, wondered if increasing the honorarium would accelerate the process. The program was six years old at that time. The subject often re-asserted itself, but the Board consistently agreed that, unless the honorarium were increased substantially, there would be little benefit from the nominal increase the Award budget would allow. It was even suggested that the Award be given every other year making it possible to double the amount of the honorarium to $20,000. The Board concluded that such action would not be prudent at that time because the Award's annual exposure was important in enhancing its recognition. Above all, there was general agreement that the main significance of the Award to the recipient and to the economic profession was the active involvement of the world's most eminent economists in the selection process, or more precisely, recognition by one's peers. Of course, the cash would also certainly be accepted with good cheer.

It was the revision of the United States income tax laws in 1986 that prompted the Award Board to increase the honorarium to $15,000. Before that, the honorarium was not subject to taxation as long as the recipient was not engaged in a "contest," but was selected without his/her prior knowledge or request. The new law specified that all honoraria would be taxed as regular income. The raising of the honorarium allowed the recipient to net $10,000 plus a little more depending on what tax bracket he/she was in.

The Award weathered well its early trials. With the passing of the first three years, the program successfully absorbed start-up uncertainties, adjusted to new academic sponsorship and began earnestly to make its mark in the world of economics.

The Selection Committees were composed of well-known economists from academia, economic associations and from past Award recipients. Now numbering five, its members serve for two years with the possibility of another two-year term at the Board's discretion.

Though all Committees were fortified by the presence and input of the most competent economists, the Committee of 1987 was likely the most star-studded, at least up to this writing. Though Nobel Laureates served on previous Committees, there were three on the 1987 Committee: James Buchanan, Robert M. Solow and James Tobin. Other 1987 Committee members were Irving Kristol and J. Randolph Rice.

At this time, the Board continues to be made up of P. K. Seidman; James H. Daughdrill, Jr., President of Rhodes College; the Chair of the Rhodes Department of Economics; a former member of the President's Council of Economic Advisors; the current or incoming President of the American Economic Association; the Chair of the Economic Club of Memphis, and Richard Gillett of Grand Rapids, Michigan. Ex officio members are Kurt F. Flexner who, because of his close association with and knowledge of the Award, is Consultant to the Board; and, Mel G. Grinspan, Director.

•FOUR•

The Recipients

GUNNAR KARL MYRDAL–1974

The Award's first recipient was Gunnar Karl Myrdal, the world famous economist from Sweden. In making the presentation, Dr. R. Aaron Gordon, president-elect of the American Economic Association, characterized Myrdal as "a columnist of the first rank, a great social scientist, and not least, a warm and understanding human being. He referred to Myrdal's "pathbreaking economic analysis in Sweden; his entry into social science culminating in *An American Dilemma* and *Asian Drama: An Inquiry Into the Poverty of Nations*; his career as policy advisor and policy maker in Sweden; and finally to his recent work in criticizing the mainstream of classical and neo-classical thought."

In his remarks, Myrdal discussed the theme of his acceptance paper "What Is Political Economy?" (Highlights of the paper are included elsewhere in this volume.) He then discussed his book *An American Dilemma* and how its writing came about. He was asked to author a book on race relations in southern United States by the Carnegie Corporation. The effort resulted in influencing his entire outlook on economics. He said, "It was very popular (in the thirties and forties)...to believe that the race problem was an economic problem. But for Lord's sake...it's not simply an economic problem...It's a lot of other things which you must see as a development of the whole social system."

Myrdal determined that what he was writing was "a complete account of American civilization looked on from the point of view of the most disadvantaged group, but also that I saw things changing..." He wrote of the need for change, of the increasing consciousness amongst the entire population of that need and pointed at the conditions and the people who would help bring about change.

As the changes took place, he felt strongly that the South was building a self-confidence it had not enjoyed for a century and that, though the racial problem, when it first fermented and then exploded, was not an economic problem, there was definitely a connection between economic progress and the movement toward equality between blacks and whites. Myrdal was impressed by the changes that had taken place.

JOHN KENNETH GALBRAITH–1975

In commenting on his selection for the Award in 1975, John Kenneth Galbraith wondered what his demeanor should be as he received it and the check involved. He humorously concluded it definitely was "one of gratitude combined with what I suppose has to be said is fully requited avarice." He added that most appropriate under the circumstances would be "a line from Fitzgerald after *Omar Khayyam:*

Some for the Glories of this world, and some
Sigh for the Prophet's Paradise to come;
Ah, take the Cash, and let the Credit go,

Nor heed the rumble of a distant drum!"

Galbraith spoke about power and its increasing force in economic life. Referring to Martin Bronfenbrenner and his observation that "economics has become...one of the lesser branches of mathematics," Galbraith added "what cannot be handled by mathematical formulae must be excluded by assumption; power, to a singular degree, is one of those things." History is another.

Speaking of the then existing problems in the United States, Galbraith said, "We have been treating our recent misfortunes (the Vietnam War and its fall-out) as though they were unique." Actually, he contended, they are repetitious of historical experience—"the experience of variously motivated adventure by countries which presume to a higher wisdom, or a higher culture, or a higher economic development in lands distant from their own." Galbraith elaborated on this thesis in his acceptance paper which is highlighted in another part of this book.

Frank E. Seidman's son, L. William Seidman, (then in the Gerald Ford White House, and now Chairman of the Federal Deposit Insurance Corporation) presented the Award to Galbraith saying that the Award is being bestowed "in recognition of your noteworthy contributions to the literature and advancement of political economy; for your consummate presentations of a modern view of the economic system...; for your penetrating critique of the forces involved in our national economic planning; for your staunchly proclaimed economic reforms covering fiscal and monetary policies and public welfare economics."

KENNETH E. BOULDING–1976

In 1976, Kenneth E. Boulding was the recipient of the Award. He had received broad professional and academic fame for his work in economics as it was related to sociology and the bureaucracy in general. In his acceptance remarks, the professor from the University of Colorado spoke of his worries about the energy problem which was at the forefront of concern in 1976. "We found a treasure chest when we discovered petroleum," he said. "We've been living off that accumulated energy capital ever since and now it's about to run out. I think we will be poorer in 2100, to put it bluntly, than we are now." Boulding foresaw "strains on the political and economic system which may result in 'little catastrophies.' "On the whole, I'm in favor of minor shock treatments. You get aging in organizations just like you do in people. They need to be revitalized." Is it possible Boulding also foresaw the frantic take-overism of the 80's?

Boulding's Award was presented by John Meyer, President of the National Bureau of Economic Research. Meyer began fascetiously by wondering what a political economist was and, having solved that problem at the Selection Committee meeting, "those on the Committee then had to decide what kind of a political economist did the committee wish to bestow the Award on." Having reached a consensus, as all Committees have, it began the serious work of deliberating. It concluded that Boulding had in a most effective and far-reaching manner made great contributions to the improvement of public policy, to the advancement of economics as a science and, finally, to the process of thinking about problems beyond economics. In his book *Beyond Economics*, Boulding specifically states, "It is hardly an exaggeration to say that the ultimate answer to every economic problem lies in some other field."

THOMAS CROMBLE SCHELLING–1977

The first recipient named after the move to Rhodes College was Thomas Cromble Schelling, Professor of Economics at

Harvard. In his acceptance speech, the 1977 recipient urged more economists to become involved in social issues confronting the United States. He called on them to use methods they have developed to solve financial problems to solve social problems such as abortion, right-to-die laws or laws restricting self-destructive behavior. "Sometimes economics is not the most intriguing, critical issue, but there are other issues belonging to no specific discipline in which economists might be able to help." Schelling emphasized that "these things are no longer beyond the realm of economic study."

Lawrence Klein, Professor of Economics and Finance, Wharton School, University of Pennsylvania, and later named Nobel Laureate in Economics, presented the Award to Schelling. Klein described Schelling's career as made of three components: first, his distinguished career mainly in mainstream economics; second, his concerns with strategy, armaments and arms control; and, third, his contributions to the studies of crime, discrimination, health and a continuing concern with strategic matters.

ARTHUR F. BURNS–1978

In 1978, Arthur F. Burns was named Award recipient. The announcement was made shortly after he left his post as Chairman of the Federal Reserve Board and prior to his being named United States Ambassador to West Germany. One of the most visible economists in the world, Burns was a giant in the formulation of United States economic policy during his 8 years as head of the Federal Reserve Board. Prior to that he served in highly influential capacities to every President from Kennedy through Ford.

In his acceptance speech, Burns decried the influence of inflation which had hovered around 7.5% in 1978. In *Southwest-*

ern Today, the Rhodes College weekly, Burns was quoted as saying, "Restrictive monetary and fiscal policies are a direct means of attacking the problem, but by themselves might unsettle the economy by bringing on extensive unemployment."

Burns received his Award on September 21, 1978, from two people: L. William Seidman, then Executive Vice-President of the Phelps-Dodge Corporation, who made only a brief presentation because his traveling schedule required an early departure, and more formally from Winton Blount, former Postmaster General of the United States and member of the Board of Trustees of Rhodes College.

The citation given to Burns referred to his pioneering work in the area of business cycles and his analysis and advocacy of the relevance of monetary policy; to his outstanding work as a teacher and as a public servant, elder statesman and central banker. In his acceptance remarks, Burns spoke of the free enterprise system from the viewpoints of Joseph Schumpeter and Karl Marx. He observed that both wrote of the decline of capitalism, that Marx foresaw it as a result of the system's failures, Schumpeter because of its successes. Burns, an ardent supporter of the free enterprise system, leaned in Schumpeter's direction for one over-riding reason: the expanding role of government in economic life. He did not embrace all of Schumpeter's views by any means, but he recognized their viability if government continued making inroads into the peoples' independence.

ARTHUR OKUN–1979

The recipient in 1979 was the late Arthur Okun, who said that the "two greatest honors in my life were being named Chairman of the Council of Economic Advisers (in President Lyndon Johnson's administration) and receiving the Seidman Award."

In an editorial of September 29, 1979, *The Commercial Appeal* spoke of the difficulty the layman has in understanding economics, "a distant blend of science and art." But "one economist who helps bring about a better understanding is Dr. Arthur Okun...he helped translate theories into practice, but his concern has not been solely with esoteric models which seem like so much mumbo-jumbo to most outsiders. He is also an observer of the outside world. He calculates economic behavior by the human equation as well as by the slide rule. He is concerned with what is fair as well as what is efficient."

In accepting the Award, Okun said the $10,000 honorarium would allow him "to do a little less speech-making and consulting than last year and a little more thinking at the Brookings Institution" where he was a Senior Fellow.

In presenting the Award to Okun, Robert Solow thought back to earlier days when both were economic advisers to the Kennedy Administration. "What struck me back in 1961 was his (Okun) terrific grasp of the order of magnitude. Art knew numbers where the rest of us only had suspicions...This way with numbers led him to find ways to approximately measure what he called the potential output of the economy so that we have a sensible target to aim at...That same feeling for numbers and the measurement of 'potential output' led to the famous Okun's Law calculation which is still in use, with minor modifications, as a way of grasping the relation between production and employment in the economy as a whole." Solow summed up his high opinion of Okun by citing the incident in which he was asked to write a letter to the President of Yale University supporting Okun's promotion to full professor. "I composed what I think was a masterpiece of brevity and effectiveness," said Solow. "I wrote: Dear Sirs: Please let me know if you don't promote him; an offer from MIT will be in the mail."

ALBERT O. HIRSCHMAN–1980

Albert O. Hirschman, Professor of Social Science at the Institute of Advanced Studies, Princeton, New Jersey, was named 1980 Award recipient. Hirschman had spent years studying the development process and in his work emphasized the interplay of politics, social processes and economics in the evolution of developing nations. Hirschman has asserted many times that morality should play a far more important role in the study and application of economics. In the historical practice of economics, morality was discarded. "Self interest was enough. Now it is becoming evident that things will not work if morality is not included," he wrote.

As did the others, who received their Awards during the economically troubled times of the late 70's and early 80's, Hirschman pointed to the inflation problems of those years and used it as an example to argue his thesis. "Inflation," he said, " is the result of special interest groups fighting themselves. They need to come back. You need benevolence between all social groups." He added that "benevolence is not to be scoffed at and that economists would do well to study altruism."

Frank W. Schiff, then Vice-President and Chief Economist of The Committee for Economic Development, presented the Award to Hirschman. He said, "Albert Hirschman is a political economist in the best sense of the word. He has been able to draw to an exceptional degree not only on economics and political science, but also anthropology, sociology, history, and psychology." Schiff spoke of Hirschman's famous book *Exit, Voice, and Loyalty* in which he developed an elaborate general theory "to explain what determined the quality of economic performance and helps explain the declines of forms, organization, and states." Or as Hirschman himself explains it, "the concepts in this theory provide a unified way of analyzing issues as diverse as economic competition, the two-party system, divorce and the American character, black power, and the failure of unhappy top officials to resign over major political issues."

RICHARD A. MUSGRAVE–1981

The 1981 recipient was Richard A. Musgrave, Adjunct Professor of the University of California, Santa Cruz, and former Professor of Political Economy at Harvard. In his acceptance remarks at the Award banquet, he expressed doubts about the effectiveness of combining large tax cuts with sweeping budget cuts. He was referring to the economic strategy initiated by President Ronald Reagan early in his administration. Musgrave did not believe that the Reagan formula would work because, "by combining tax with expenditure cuts, the administrators chose to forego the inflation check which would have resulted had expenditures only been cut." He asked Congress to reconsider its tax policy and to postpone tax reductions until the budget could absorb them. To battle inflation, Musgrave favored some form of incomes policy such as wage and price guidelines.

Musgrave explained that his interest in public policy and especially in the budget's role in the democratic process were his prime attraction to economics.

William Baumol presented the Award to Musgrave. He spoke of the recipient's books on public finance and said "they have changed the outlines of the field...every writer on the subject must refer to their contents. Generations of graduate students have grown up under their teachings. Richard Musgrave is truly a man of distinction."

JANOS KORNAI–1982

In 1982, the Award again went outside the borders of the

United States, marking another major step in its climb to international recognition. Chosen for the Award was Janos Kornai, head of the Insitute of Economics, Hungarian Academy of Sciences in Budapest. Kornai is a distinguished author of many books and articles. His early work, *Overcentralizations in Economics Administration*, had a marked influence on the thinking of Hungarian intellectuals which culminated in the uprising of 1955. Kornai was particularly candid during his visit to Memphis. When it came to so-called sacred economic theories in both the East and the West, he as much as said, "A plague on both your houses." In his acceptance remarks, Kornai, instead of prescribing a remedy to solve the world's economic ills, prescribed mainly for his colleagues in the economics profession. As was written in an editorial in *The Commercial Appeal* September 27, 1972 "(Kornai) says that all economists are overconfident to the point of arrogance, that they should 'refrain from the cocksureness of the fanatic quacks' and sincerely confess to the limits of their knowledge.' The economic doctors should realize what the medical doctors have learned, that the therapeutic value of any prescription must be balanced against the side effects that may result from its application. The bottom line is "Which kind of a disease do you choose if perfect health is unattainable?"

The Award to Kornai was presented by Arthur Bayer, first Director of the Award and, at that time, Dean of Undergraduate Studies at Babson College. Bayer said, "This man's (Kornai) ability to analyze objectively the economic efficiency of various systems, whether price determined or centrally directed, is a credit to his unwavering quest for what is real. The relationship between theory and realism, between what is possible and what is daydreaming are questions addressed throughout the many written words of our recipient. With logical clarity, he dissects, examines, evaluates, and criticizes the idealized economic models created by economic/political forces in the world."

ROBERT M. SOLOW–1983

Robert Solow had been closely associated with the Award and with Rhodes College (as a visiting lecturer) for a number of years. He served on the Award Board of Trustees in 1979 and 1980 and later on the Selection Committee in 1986 and 1987. It was in 1983, however, that he was chosen Award recipient. In 1987, he was named Nobel Laureate in Economics. He is Institute Professor of Economics at Massachusetts Institute of Technology and a widely published expert on economic theory, economic development and the economics of exhaustible resources. As reported in *Southwestern Today*, April 30, 1983, "Dr. Solow is known for his advances in economic thought. He developed many of the tools that practical economists use when they grapple with the long-term development problems of less developed countries. In the 1950's, he wrote a series of papers on the factors affecting growth of national income which provided the theoretical foundation of what is now standard economic analysis."

A past Chairman of the Federal Reserve Bank of Boston, he suggested during his Memphis visit that the Fed should publicly set its projections for growth in the economy. Such knowledge would be a major influence in coordinating fiscal and monetary policy. He further stated that added to the Fed's projections on Gross National Product should be those from the Congressional Budget Office and from the President–a remedy to help resolve the constant tugging between the makers of fiscal policy and the makers of monetary policy. "The Fed would no doubt prefer not to be so explicit (in making public its GNP projections)," said Solow in an article in *The Commercial Appeal*, September 30,

1983, "The guardians of the mystery always prefer smoke and dim light."

This time the honor of presenting the Award to the recipient went to Marshall E. McMahon, then Chair, Department of Economics and Business Adminstration of Rhodes College, and a member of the Award's Board. In his presentation, McMahon said, "Dr. Solow's internationally recognized contributions to economic thought have not only extended boundaries of our knowledge of economic theory, they have also improved our ability to formulate and execute public policy. Indeed, his contributions to economics are to be found in his approach and method as well as the substance of his work. It is interesting to note that one measure of Dr. Solow's success, of the contributions he has made to economics as judged by his peers, is the fact that one is hard put to find a textbook of economic theory, even at the undergraduate level, that does not make reference to his work."

JAMES M. BUCHANAN–1984

The Award selection pendulum took a swing to the right in 1984 when James Buchanan was named recipient. Head of the Center for Study of Public Choice at George Mason University, he agreed strongly with many of the Ronald Reagan presidency's economic opinions. The thrust of his work revolves about "the public choice theory." It applies mathematics and other economic methodologies to the problems and institutions of political science. The prevailing thought is that public choice is the doctrine of the "invisible foot," an opposite concept to Adam Smith's "invisible hand." Smith believed that, in the pursuit of their own good, individuals produced benefits for society at large. Public choice asserts that this same self-interest results in harmful government interference in the economy. More to the point, public choice argues that government interference is in no way beneficial and that, as Reagan said, "the less government, the better."

"An economist, he is also a citizen who praises the values of individualism, liberty, and democracy," said Marvin DeVries when he presented the Award to Buchanan in 1984. DeVries was Dean of the Frank E. Seidman Graduate Business School, Grand Valley State University in Allendale, Michigan, a widely-heralded institution named in memory of the same man for whom the Award is named. DeVries continued, "Government is necessary, Buchanan believes, adding, however, as did Adam Smith, David Hume, and America's founding fathers, that prudence teaches that constitutional checks must be imposed on the exercise of governmental power if liberty is to be preserved. In our own times, Buchanan contends, additional constitutional provisions are needed if the days of deficit, spending and appalling public debt are to be ended."

In *The Calculus of Consent*, Buchanan and Gordon Tullock wrote, "...we share the faith that man can rationally organize his own society, that existing organizations can always be perfected, and that nothing in the social order should remain exempt from rational, critical, and intelligent discussion."

In 1986, Buchanan was named Nobel Laureate in Economics.

GARY S. BECKER–1985

An "authentic genius" was how Nobel Laureate George Stigler described Gary S. Becker, who received the Award in 1985. Becker, Chairman of the Department of the Economics at the University of Chicago, is a prime representative of the "Chicago School of Economics," a term used to characterize a conservative stance on economic matters which was nourished at the University of Chicago. Becker also teaches sociology, which, in combination with economics, has given him insights that well serve his pioneering use of economic and statistical analyses in his approach to socio-economic studies. The *Memphis Daily News* on September 23, 1985, stated, "His 1964 book *Human Capital* transformed the field of labor economics. In *Economics of Discrimination*, he analyzes the cause and effects of discrimination in employment and earnings. In other words, he explores the economics of crime and punishment, the allocation of time, fertility and even suicide."

The Boston Globe has called Becker "the practical progenitor of that branch of economics known as human capital, meaning the analysis of investment in the education and skills of a nation's population."

When Becker received his Award, it was presented by Walter P. Armstrong, Jr., a prominent Memphis attorney who was Chairman of the Economic Club of Memphis, a co-host of the Award banquet.

Becker received the Award, in part Armstrong said, "because of his distinguished contributions to economics and the social sciences by creatively showing students and peers the value of using economic theory and concepts to analyze various types of human behavior and institutions."

AMARTYA K. SEN–1986

On pages 346 and 347 of the book, *Who's Who in Economics* edited by Mark Blaug and Paul Sturges (MIT Press, 1983), is a capsulized biography of Amartya Sen. In addition to listing his vital statistics, degrees, contributions and other salient facts, it notes that Sen was Drummond Professor of Political Economy at All Souls College, the University of Oxford, England. Directly under Sen's biography is that of William Nassau Senior

(1790-1864) who was also Drumond Professor at the same college from 1825-1830.

The coincidence goes beyond the accident of alphabetical listing. Both professors were and are distinguished representatives of their profession and occupied the same chair, considered to be the oldest in the economics discipline.

Sen, a native of India, received his Award in 1986 and was the third recipient from outside the United States.

In their book, Blaug and Sturges report Sen's principal contributions as being "works in welfare economics and social choice theory, particularly in expanding their informational bases, incorporating considerations of liberty and rights, and exploring problems of collective rationality." The list is much longer and includes references to Sen's work on the choice of technology in developing countries' methods of shadow pricing and the development of a theory on the causes of famine.

These achievements of Sen were discussed in a warmer manner when Nobel Laureate Robert Solow presented the Award to Sen. He said, "The fact that economics has a thousand ways to talk about efficiency and none to talk about equity sometimes attracts strange people to economics and directs them to strange problems. Amartya Sen's influence is a counterweight in the opposite direction. There is a direct line but a line that is not often traveled from Professor Sen's early work on economic development and growth to his most recent work which is as much philosophy as it is economics."

Since having received the Award, Sen has become Lamont University Professor at Harvard.

WILLIAM J. BAUMOL–1987

At the time he received the Award in 1987, William J. Baumol held the joint appointment as professor of Economics at

Princeton University and New York University. When asked how he did that, he intimated that it was not easy, but so enjoyable, challenging and stimulating. He was also Director of the E. V. Starr Center for Applied Economics at NYU.

In making the presentation, Marina Whitman, Vice-President of General Motors Corporation and a former member of the Award's Board of Trustees, referred to the breadth of Baumol's intellectual interests. "From market structure to welfare theory, from electrical utility pricing to the economics of the performing arts, there is virtually no area of microeconomics that his fertile mind has not touched and advanced. Will Baumol's work displays an originality so rich that he has often been forced to coin new words to describe his ideas, words like "contestability" or "superfairness" because the existing dictionary cannot encompass them."

While she praised other facets of his accomplishments by specific mentions of his successful outreach to business and to the arts, Dr. Whitman also emphasized Baumol's "gifts as a teacher (which) go far beyond clarity and brilliance of exposition. In his enthusiasm for his subject, his insistence that analytical rigor can serve as the handmaiden rather than the opponent of human engagement, and the enduring kindness and concern he displays toward personal difficulties, he breathes new life into the hackneyed adjective 'inspiring.' And, if an educator is ultimately judged by the quality and accomplishments of his students, the list of Will's former pupils is sufficient to assure him an honored place among economists of all generations."

ROBERT TRIFFIN–1988

Once again the Selection Committee and the Board reached across the ocean, this time to honor Robert Triffin of Belgium in 1988. Triffin was chosen for a number of reasons, a most important one being his work in behalf of international monetary reform and regional monetary integration. He played a leading role in the conception and negotiation of the *European Payments Union* and of the *European Monetary System*. He continues to cooperate in the studies aimed at promoting the evolution of the *EMS* toward the full *Economic and Monetary Union* envisaged as an ultimate goal by its creators and by the *Action Committee for the United States of Europe* of Jean Monnet, with whom he collaborated closely for many years.

Nobel Laureate James Tobin, who made the presentation, focused on this part of Triffin's work when he said, "...but Robert has never favored an inward-looking protectionist Europe. He would like to see a world-wide central bank, and other global institutions, particularly devoted to improving the lot of the Third World. And above all, Robert seeks world peace, disarmament, and detente."

Continuing on this theme in an interview with *The Commercial Appeal* on Friday, September 16, 1988, Triffin said, "The present monetary system has led the United States to amass a $500 billion dollar debt to foreigners, promoted the arms race, fueled inflation and funneled capital away from nations that need it most." He noted the decreasing flow of dollars to debtor nations from the United States and that, though they resulted in reduced inflation, it caused the U.S. to build a staggering debt. Another result was the creation of a problem of social justice. "The richest country in the world, with the least need for capital, is absorbing the savings of countries that are much poorer and more in need of capital that the U.S."

In his presentation remarks on Triffin, Tobin closed by saying, "No one could be better qualified for the Award for an economist who has distinguished himself internationally to the interdisciplinary advancement of economic thought as it applies to the implementation of public policy." Tobin was quoting from the Award criteria.

HERBERT STEIN–1989

At this writing (Spring, 1989) the Award ceremony at which Herbert Stein will receive the Award is scheduled for September 14, 1989. The presentation will be made by Paul McCracken, Edmund Ezra Day Distinguished University Professor Emeritus at The University of Michigan, an early participant in the Award program and currently a member of its Board.

It is quite likely that press reports will elaborate on his contributions to economics as written, in part, in his Award citation: for "your efforts to improve the quality of the public sector in the economy; for your commitment to national and sound fiscal policy; for your contribution to the public of a better understanding of economic issues..." The item referring to explaining economic issues to layman is well documented by Stein's articles in *The Wall Street Journal* and many other publications and in his books, the latest of which is *Governing the Five Trillion Dollar Economy* (Oxford Press, 1989). At the time the Award to Stein was announced, he was consultant to the Congressional Budget Office and to the State Department on the economy of Israel, and Senior Fellow at the American Enterprise Institute.

The Future

Even as the arrangements are being completed for the 1989 Award presentation, the machinery is in motion for the selection of the next one, the seventeenth. The first sixteen were, for the most part, older economists some of whose contributions were first noted almost a half-century ago. There are still many eminent economists in this group who are constantly being considered for the Award.

Yet, there is another group of economists, younger by most professional standards, who are making their marks and will be the stars of the future in terms of their contributions to economics and the recognition they will receive. It is from members of this group that future Selection Committees will find themselves choosing recipients. And to the everlasting benefit of the Award, it will be members of this group who will assume the guidance of the Award, who will fire the debate on what is political economy and who are the political economists.

As is revealed in their acceptance papers, many recipients have asked for a broader, more humanistic approach to economics–an approach that also takes into account the reality of the human condition, its success, its failures, its travails–all the factors that are difficult, if not impossible, to quantify. Perhaps some of the younger economists have taken heed to the older generation. They celebrate the wedding of economics and policy believing that each noble component is worthy of the other. Then there are other economists and social scientists who foresee no future for the union, that there is no true affinity of the elements involved. And there are those in all disciplines who wonder if the marriage can withstand the tribulations of outside interference and inside petulance.

So the debate continues. It may be in the continuation that lies the real essence of this member of the "dismal science." Policy and economics. Political economics. Perhaps it is not a wedding, only an accommodation.

FIVE

Highlights of The Recipients' Acceptance Papers

GUNNAR KARL MYRDAL–1974
Selection Committee: P. K. Seidman, Kurt F. Flexner, Marvin G. DeVries

What is Political Economy?

Early economists, called political scientists, believed they should draw policy conclusions on rational grounds. They also believed policy conclusions could be drawn from theory which they defined in narrow terms and which was very abstract in the Ricardian mode. They maintiained those conclusions must be based on knowledge of other subjects. Later, economists perfected "welfare economics" and "welfare theory," which was based on modern philosophy and hedonistic psychology, both of which eventually became obsolete resulting in an isolation of economists. Myrdal subscribed strongly to the view that contrary to the practices of the "new" economists, "we must observe many other things in this world in order to draw plausible conclusions." Myrdal believed that development means a change in the whole social system, that change is logical and necessary because there are interrelations between different factors in the system. He stated that in the near future economists would be political scientists, that they will consider factors other than economics in their conclusions.

The "welfare theorists," heirs of the neo-classical economists whose roots were in utilitarian moral philosophy, were left behind by professional philosophers and psychologists. "Modern establishment economists have stayed with welfare theory but have tried to lose its foundation in an obsolete moral philosophy and psychology. They miss "the historical perspective they should gain by intensive studies of their predecessors and, at the same time, the awareness they could get by such studies of where the basic difficulties are buried."

Myrdal insisted upon the necessity of setting forth instrumental value premises. Doing so serves three purposes: (1) it determines in a rational way the statement of problems, (2) it forms a logical basis for reaching rational policy, (3) it helps to eliminate the scientific investigation of "distorting biases." However, Myrdal said he has not "reached a final and fully satisfactory solution...of how to ascertain the value premises needed in research...and when drawing policy conclusions."

JOHN KENNETH GALBRAITH–1975
Selection Committee: P. K. Seidman, Kurt F. Flexner, Gunnar Myrdal

On History, Political Economy, and Vietnam

The increasing influence of the modern corporation and modern trade unions as instruments for the exercise of economic power, is being excluded from economics as we know it today. Because power is one of those factors that cannot be handled mathematically, it seems to be automatically excluded from economic purview. Galbraith hoped that a preoccupation with history could also be added back to economic consideration. Together, the better understanding of power and history would not only enhance our comprehension of economics, but also improve our view of foreign policy. The lack of such has caused us to treat "our recent misfortunes, the Vietnam war, as though they were unique."

For 900 years, Western Europeans repeatedly attempted to extend their influence to lesser races by warring excursions. All those efforts had 3 features in common: "(1) An avowed spiritual, cultural, moral or other civilized benefit for the people toward whom the effort was directed, (2) all have involved some economic interest, (3) all have ended in failure." The United States experience in Vietnam was no different. In the historic fashion, there was "an admixture of idealism and economic interest. Freedom from discipline and coercion were the foundations of our efforts. As for economic interest, though there was little indication that one of our motives was profit-inspired, there is little evidence that profit per se was an important consideration in our Vietnam expedition. Rather economic interest was served by our wishing to preserve free enterprise in the U.S. by attempting to preserve it everywhere."

On the other hand, Hanoi, our adversary, was treated more wisely by the Russians and the Chinese; they sent no troops, no advisers. "There was a Pentagon East, but no Kremlin East." Their influence was great, but almost on a non-personal basis. Galbraith adds, however, that where the Communists resorted to the same process as we did, as in Yugoslavia, Egypt, Algeria, for example, they suffered the same experience as we did in Vietnam.

Not the "uncontrollable imperialist drive for markets, for

outlets, for investment."–none of these were behind our Vietnam encounter, as was held by certain leftists, according to Galbraith. The overriding cause was most likely our "inability to be guided by historical experience."

The grave errors of the men responsible for Vietnam notwithstanding, our system prevailed and we withdrew. "It came out of the good sense of the country as a whole." Galbraith said, "There were elements of greatness in the way the nation corrected the errors of the leaders on Vietnam." He asked, "Does it not say something for democracy?"

KENNETH E. BOULDING–1976

Selection Committee: P. K. Seidman, John Meyer,
Eleanor Bernert Sheldon,
Kermit Gordon, Kurt Flexner

Adam Smith as an Institutional Economist

"Adam Smith is both the Adam and the Smith of economics, the father and the forger," begins Boulding. The seeds of almost everything that has happened in economics can be traced back to him. With the exception of such as marginal utility and explicit marginal analysis, though he did not discover them, Boulding believes Smith came very close to doing so. It was not unusual, then, for him to wonder whether "there is anything in Adam Smith which foreshadows the institutional economics of Veblen, Commons "and corresponding movements elsewhere. Institutional economics was a widespread, rumbling, somewhat underground critique of neoclassical economic orthodoxy, particularly in the United States and Western Europe...from about 1880 to 1920. One would identify it as idealogically to the left, but by no means Marxist."

Boulding lists six complaints of the institutional economists against orthodox economics (1) lack of empirical base for economic theory, not interested enough in the complexities of the real world, (2) lack of dynamics because it was obsessed with equilibrium and equilibrium theories, (3) it depended on a "highly atomistic, individualistic psychology which left no place for human learning and socialization," (4) it does not give recognition to the role of society not only to human behavior but to economic activity, (5) "lack of attention...to the existence of community as a network of relationships and identities," (6) orthodox economics isolates pieces of the total social system and studies it without considering their relationship to the total.

Boulding leans heavily on Veblen for his thesis. He speaks of his criticism of *a priori* preference, simple maximizing behavior and the concept of conspicuous consumption; yet, Boulding wonders why Veblen denies the reality of the symbolic nature of many economic goods. Likening Veblenian economics to the parable of the prodigal son, Boulding characterizes Veblen's professional and personal life as having an inclination to "return to the solid puritan and Norwegian virtues of engineering and the family farm." Veblen's quarrel with the view that labor is "a mere discommodity which has to be paid for in wages" is based on his concept of the "instinct of workmanship." Boulding, on the other hand, explains that Veblen's use of "instinct" is a semantic indulgence and that human interest in work is learned and not the result of gene structure. There is an agreement, however, that, instinctive or not, humans are constantly active; "some of this activity we value for its own sake, some...because of its products..."

Boulding then reckons how Adam Smith would fare as an institutional economist in light of the six characteristics listed above (1) Adam Smith scores well in his concern for the empirical base of economics with the type of data collection and analysis available in his day. Smith's empiricism was evident, though it may have been based more on insight than elaboration of method. (2) In terms of dynamism in economics, Boulding says Adams also scores high. *The Wealth of Nations* is dominated by the dynamic evolutionary approach. "(Adam Smith) is always talking about what happens in the 'progress of society.' " Especially was Smith sensitive to the learning process in the dynamics of human society. He associated that thought with productivity, the increase in dexterity, the saving of time, and, eventually, with the development of machinery. (3) Regarding the matter of individualistic psychology, in maximizing behavior, Boulding believes Smith thought that people do what they think is best at the time. "What is 'best,' however, may include benevolence and moral sentiment as well as the most outrageously selfish of motivations." (4) In the matter of "taking explicit account of the role of institutions and organizations in society,... he was well aware of the importance of organizations and of the fact that they interact with each other." (5) With regard to the theory of community, "*The Wealth of Nations* perhaps does not have a great deal to say, but *The Theory of Moral Sentiments* may yet turn out to be the seminal work of a whole theory of integrative systems." It was in that work, Boulding reminds us, that Smith first mentions "the invisible hand," but in context different from the popularly accepted one of how the mechanism by which exchange and the price system operate. (6) On the necessity for a general social science, Boulding says Smith "has strong claims for being a pioneer sociologist." Scattered throughout *The Wealth of Nations* are discussions of the "various political limitations on the general doctrine of natural liberty."

Boulding finishes his paper by acclaiming Smith to have been a political economist. Smith, he maintains, stood on this principle: "Government not only should prevent the beneficial effects of liberty to flower by not hindering itself with unnecessary duties, but it also has the obligation to check the excesses of natural liberty and see that it does not produce defective monetary systems, defective public goods or defective human beings."

THOMAS CROMBLE SCHELLING–1977
Selection Committee: P. K. Seidman, H. Scott Gordon,
Eleanor Bernert Sheldon,
Gilbert Steiner, Spence Wilson

On Exercising Choice

As did Gunnar Myrdal, Schelling asked, "What is political economy?" He suggested two answers: (1) economics in the context of policy, (2) political economy is "any problem to whose solution an economist can bring a little insight... in finding a solution or facing an issue, even though the problem would not be identified as economics."

Within the context of the latter, Schelling provides a personal answer by discussing three topics in which he was involved.

First, the supposition that people could choose the sex of their children. We now can choose, as a result of modern technology, whether to have children at all. If we could choose sex because of added technology, Schelling's interest is not in the technology but in the consequences. Technology is not to be ignored, however. Who controls it, is it subject to error, can it be miscalculated–these and many other related questions are certainly pertinent.

Most people are unprepared to make a choice of the sex of

their children. It is not only a new and strange experience, but any decision would be based on the makeup of their experiences with their families. There is the additional factor of how their culture views boys or girls and what values are placed on each. Too, social and demographic influences must be considered along with possible governmental interdiction to meet national needs for one sex or the other. The decision that would be parents would make would be colored by many factors.

The effect on total populations could be awesome. Fads or temporary inclinations could result in unmanageable imbalances in sex ratio. Higher ratios of males in one area, lower ratios of females in other areas could cause shifts difficult to reconcile. If so, the government might attempt to stabilize the birth ratio by various measures which may or may not be acceptable to various constituencies.

The social and constitutional implications are also indescribable. It appears that even if opportunities for sex-choice were to become possible, the problems would be unlimited. "So it isn't only parents who might like to be spared some of the choices that would have to be made if this particular technology became available. There are some things—the weather may be one and the sex of a child at birth another—that are a great relief to be unable to control. The birth lottery dispenses arbitrary justice indiscriminately, but it may beat having to discriminate."

Schelling's second topic is addictive behavior with emphasis on smoking. Most smokers would like to quit. As in all addictions, however, there is a part of them that is constantly rationalizing why it is not necessary. If in the case of smoking, cigarettes could be made impossible to obtain, and if people could vote on that action, indications are that smokers would vote overwhelmingly in favor.

Tobacco with food and possibly alcohol "represent distinct

issues in social control." Nearly everyone who wants heroin suppressed is not an addict. And not many people who take heroin are pleading to be deprived of it. But tens of millions of people wish they could smoke less, or quit smoking, and the primary constituency for social action against cigarettes is probably not among the non-smokers but among those who smoke.

Schelling explains he is not bringing a solution, "but only trying to identify a problem in social control that is particularly difficult in a democracy–the possibility that people want to be forcibly protected from their own bad habits." Schelling said it is likely medical research would make dramatic advances in improving health and prolonging life, but most of that would focus on how to better care for ourselves. "The easy part is being intellectually persuaded. The hard part is learning how to make ourselves do it."

The third topic is "exercising the right to die." Schelling proposes "that one useful viewpoint for examining 'the right to die' is that it is our right, not somebody else's." In that posture, he represents the consumer and asks "what institutional arrangements would I like to govern my dying?" If there were a number of "regimes" for dying, we would choose a death style as we choose a lifestyle.

The consumer viewpoint also allows a person to decide how much personal sacrifice one is willing to make in terms of suffering, inconvenience and cost as they relate to their effects on family and friends.

One could demand, "Let me die," "Help me die," and "Make me die." The last raises the issue of one having arranged for death prior to reaching a stage where, because of resurfaced fear or derangement, one demonstrates terror at dying and asks not to have that terror prolonged. There is the one who rationally planned one's death under certain circumstances and there is the one who denies that plan and demands to supersede the first one. Which is the authentic one? Schelling draws a parallel between the above example and a first-time parachutist. "Which is the authentic individual, the one who grips the door-frame until his knuckles turn white, desperately resisting the foot against his back, or the one that said, on the ground a few minutes earlier, to use all the strength you need to get him out and not mistake his phobia for himself?"

Both "Let me die" and "Help me die" raise tortuous issues and "are laden with potential anxiety, conflict, misunderstanding, suspicion, guilt and mistrust." It places great burdens on the person agreeing to be your accessory. The decisions to act as per the dying person's request and your understanding with that person can be a burden too great to bear.

Schelling concludes by stating that the "least burdensome kind of help and the least devisive would probably be participation in the arrangements we might make together, while death is still remote and hypothetical, for a decent death in certain contingencies. The ideal methodology, he proposes, is a science-fiction one—"a diagnostic contrivance, implanted in the brain, that in the event of a cerebral hemorrhage, would measure the severity, remaining inactive if the predicted paralyses was below some limiting value but fatally aggravating the condition above that limit." He suggests the principle would be attractive to many and probably unattractive to others, in keeping with his consumer approach to the subject.

ARTHUR F. BURNS–**1978**

Selection Committee: P. K. Seidman, H. Scott Gordon,
Eleanor Bernert Sheldon,
Frank Schiff, Spence Wilson

The Future of the Free Enterprise System

Karl Marx said that capitalism contained the seeds of its own destruction and would be replaced by socialism. Joseph Schumpeter agreed. Marx, however, believed capitalism would fall because of its failures, Schumpeter because of its successes. In elaborating, Burns said that the "nations practicing socialism in Marx's and Schumpeter's sense had either banished free enterprise under external military pressure, or had undergone an internal revolution without ever developing a significant degree of free enterprise." Second, those countries practicing free enterprise had greater economic success than where it was prohibited or severely limited. Third, experience has discredited Marx's analysis while Schumpeter's theory "that capitalism would eventually be destroyed by its successes in improving the lot of the people cannot be dismissed so readily."

Of special interest in this regard was Burn's concern over the "expanding role of government in economic life...The spread of political democracy has accentuated the trend toward seeking governmental solutions of economic and social problems." He pointed to statistics demonstrating the expanding activities and cost of increasing government presence. The result is the growing burden of taxation from every government and the increase of Federal budget deficits.

The inevitable result of that combination is inflation. Inflation is a serious threat to the free enterprise system. Not only does it distort business' perspective of its profits, it erodes purchasing power, undermines desire to save, drives up interest rates, creates uncertainty, weakens capital markets as investors leave the stock markets. The erosion in equity issues makes it increasingly difficult for even the most substantial corporations to finance their long term investment projects.

Not only has inflation "weakened the framework of our economic system...there is even greater reason for concern about its impact on social and political institutions." It leads to recession and unemployment, both of which are generally followed by more government intervention.

Burns noted that neither Marx or Schumpeter mentioned inflation as a cause of capitalism's downfall, but he wondered if the results of inflation "may not be reinforcing the very processes on which (Schumpeter) dwelt so provocatively."

Not all of the problems facing the U.S. dynamic and prosperous economy can be blamed on inflation, but it is our main problem. Others are the tax burden, excessive government regulation, excessive power of labor, deterioration of central-city areas, decline of the work ethic and widespread crime.

"There are some faint flickerings, however, that the American people are becoming less passive about the dangers facing our nation (1978); moves on the state and local levels, a more positive attitude in Congress are examples. He urged caution, however, because "restrictive monetary and fiscal policies, if pushed far enough" not only bring inflation under control; they could "unsettle the economy by bringing about extensive unemployment."

Burn's prescription in 1978 for a balanced attack on the inflation problem included (1) a continuing moderately restrictive monetary policy by the Federal Reserve Bank, (2) the budget permit substantial cut in the Federal deficit, (3) increases in Federal employee salaries be reduced, (4) the President, all presidential appointees and Congress reduce their salaries by 10%, (5) the President ask all corporate heads to refrain from any compensation increases for two years, (6) the establishment of national production councils, (7) postpone target dates set for environmental and safety regulations.

ARTHUR M. OKUN–1979

Selection committee: Arthur Bayer, Jack Carlson,
Charles F. Phillips, Jr.,
Thomas C. Schelling, Frank W. Schiff

The Invisible Handshake and the Inflationary Process

Noting that the orthodox explanations for inflation were becoming increasingly difficult to justify–that prices rose dramatically while supply exceeded demand, that inflation continued upward in the face of a recession–Okun focused on another pertinent point: that 'in millions of instances...nonunion employers with no contractual obligations granted general pay increases when they had abundant applicants, no vacancies, and negligible quit rates." He puzzled over that, then concluded that "their behavior is sensible...(that) employers are in fact striving to minimize payroll costs *reckoned over a substantial time-horizon.*"

He attributed this phenomenon to the theory of "implicit contracts: firms with no explicit contractual obligations nonetheless act, in the pursuit of long-term profitability, to fulfill certain general commitments to their employees. They are guided by an invisible handshake, as well as by Adam Smith's invisible hand." These companies are investing in personnel relationships and seeking regulations as good employers fair to their employees. Referring to one employer who had cut back employment, raised his workers' pay by 7% while experiencing drops in sales and profits and with no union threat, Okun explained, "As a conscious policy, he did not take advantage of his workers while he had the upper hand in the labor market so he could count on their remembering his actions when the job market tightened." To bolster this point, Okun refers to the Keynesian assumption of a floor on money wages.

This same rationale carries over to many product markets. "By foregoing king-size markups in tight markets, the sellers build a clientele and establish a reputation that helps to retain customers when markets ease."

Okun extends this rationale to the price increases many industries impose as a result of cost increases. They emphasize the cost increase aspect to convince customers they are not taking advantage of a tight market. During recessions, price adjustments are influenced by decreasing costs. However, "during recent recessions, prices in customer markets have not fallen...rather they have kept rising." This is contrary to what happens in the auction markets; where the traditional supply-and-demand model is "confirmed beautifully." Prices in customer-markets and auction markets performed differently because "they are set differently–one by an impersonal mechanism that equates supply and demand continuously and the other by a managerial strategy oriented strongly toward long-term customer relationships."

Developed by macroeconomists, the theory of implicit contracts is also important to microeconomics. The mechanism for making transactions in the auction markets would be "abysmally inefficient" in customer markets. Nor can the labor market rely on the impersonal aspects of the auction markets. In the high costs of funding employment, on one hand, and of funding a productive worker on the other, there is an "implicit agreement" among both on the benefits of continuing employment. In turn, this benefit is broadened to buyer-seller relationships in assuring sellers of continued good service, reliability and predictability. "While the sellers are serving their own interests...they also improve the efficiency of the economy by reducing transaction costs."

Implicit contracts also help to explain the inflationary process. "Thus an overheated economy initially has a rosy glow from low employment rates, ebullient capital formation, and strong productivity growth." Just as inflation is slow-starting during a period of excess demand, it is slow-stopping when demand weakens.

While inflation was modest in the fifties and sixties, the seventies witnessed rapid inflation, resulting in cost increases and ultimately price increases. Okun contended that "in general, as people adapt to an inflationary world, they make inflation more rapid and more persistent." This alters implicit and explicit contracts "in ways that make inflation feed upon itself."

Implicit contracts have other effects on the cost of inflation. First, when it stems from a general, economy-wide cause, wages and prices react differently. Though "changes in relative prices and wages serve no useful function as rewards or market signals...they reshuffle income among families." Second, "because inflation can feed upon itself, an acceleration of inflation must increase uncertainty about the future course of inflation." This results in a withdrawal from asset markets, deposits, bonds and other fixed-assets. Third, the withdrawal from money undermines the sense of security and well-being of a society which has been founded upon and reliant upon its most important yardstick and means of communication.

This view "highlights the dangers of stimulative fiscal and monetary policies that permit inflation...(and) suggests the need for a consistent and determined strategy to slow the growth of aggregate spending." Monetary restraint can cure inflation but at a high cost...Implicit and explicit contracts in periods of restrictive policy, will increase unemployment and reduce output. Such an undiversified anti-inflationary program is "an inefficient, high-risk strategy. Fortunately there are ample opportunities for diversification."

The jump in oil prices imposed by OPEC offers an example. More money is being spent on petroleum, therefore less money is available for other items resulting in reduced output and employment. There is a push toward inflation and recession simultaneously. Monetary and fiscal policy stimulation is an option in combating this reaction, but that only fuels up inflation. Considering the OPEC price increase as being the same as an excise tax on consumers, it can be neutralized by a cut in state sales tax or federal payroll taxes, a strategy that "can avoid the grim alternatives of accepting recession or adding to inflation." Also, to be employed for the same purpose as cost-reducing measures would be subsidies for low-income workers as substitutes for minimum wages and the elimination of acreage controls on farm products. Another approach resulting in major anti-inflationary benefits could be to link "tax benefits of accelerated depreciation to compliance with the price and wage guidelines."

Okun concludes, "Implicit contracts help to explain why inflation is costly and why it is difficult to eliminate once it has become entrenched. But those institutions also create the opportunity for cost-reducing measures and tax-based income policies to help curb inflation, along with a consistent fiscal-monetary strategy to slow the growth of total dollar spending."

ALBERT O. HIRSCHMAN–1980

Selection Committee: Arthur A. Bayer, Martin S. Feldstein, Frank W. Schiff, Charles F. Phillips, Jr., Thomas C. Schelling

Morality and the Social Sciences: A Durable Tension

Dr. Hirschman dedicated his acceptance paper to the memory of Arthur M. Okun (1928-1980).

Though the role of moral considerations and conscience does not come easily to social scientists, Hirschman contends that there is an increased concern for these values even in economics. He refers to Machiavelli who "proclaimed he would deal with political institutions as they really exist and not with imaginary republics and monarchies governed by religious precepts and moralistic parties." Hirschman says modern political science "owes a great deal to Machiavelli's shocking claim that ordinary notions of moral behavior for individuals many not be suitable as rules of conduct for states."

From the ramifications of this arose the principle of self-interest which, a century later, gave way "to outright celebration: Adam Smith evinced no religious qualms when he bestowed praise on the Invisible Hand for enlisting self-interested behavior on behalf of social order and economic progress." Hirschman declared that the discovery of that social mechanism, "if properly unshackled is far less demanding of human nature and therefore infinitely more reliable." All of this was a continuation of the refusal to be satisfied with the traditional view of what "ought" to be done in favor of what actually "is."

When Marx entered the scene, he too consistently refused to appeal to moral argument. He maintained he was the father of "scientific socialism," but Hirschman contends that, in Marx's prediction of the eventual collapse of capitalism, he "mixed, uncannily, cold scientific propositions with hot moral outrage" and that therein was the "extraordinary appeal of his work in an age both addicted to science and starved of moral values."

There is an understandable tension between morality and analytical-scientific activity. Neither one is dependent on the other. Indeed, moral conviction may even be undermined by analytical argument. Hirschman believes the "hostility to morality is more than a birthmark of modern science" and that "anti-moralist petulance will frequently recur." In elaborating on this, Hirschman suggests that "social science is peculiarly subject to the compulsion to produce paradox." Being part of society, living in it, contributing to it, we have a tendency to think we know what goes on. For social science to get our attention, "it must come up with something that shows how badly commensense understanding has led us astray. Important social science discoveries are therefore typically counter-intuitive, shocking..."

The incursions, lately, of economists into the social areas outside the bailiwick of economics, exemplifies this interest for the morally shocking. Economic approaches have been taken to such as crime, marriage, procreation, voting, etc. The economists' emphasis, though, was on "grubby cost/benefit analysis and was bound to produce moral shock." Hirschman believes, however, that this "way of achieving notoriety and fame for the economists is running into decreasing returns "because, one, the absence of benevolence has been around long enough to create the rediscovery of the need for morality; second, "it has become increasingly clear that, in a number of important areas, the economy is in fact liable to perform poorly without a minimum of 'benevolence.' "

Benevolence was started in microeconomics. It could assert itself in the ethical behavior of the marketer toward the customer. When the marketer takes advantage of the customer, the government steps in, not necessarily successfully. But if the marketer exercises voluntary and acceptable constraints, benevolence is invoked. The fact is, though, that such voluntary action may not materialize, in which case there is market failure calling into play the need for ethical norms and behavior to "supplement and, on occasion, to supplant self-interest."

It is in the macroarea that "giant strides in the rehabilitation of morality as an essential 'input' into functioning economy have taken place...(this) as a result of the contemporary experience with, and concern over, inflation." In place of the debates on the technical reasons for inflation, Hirschman says we need to probe "deeply into the social and political underlay of the economy" for better understanding of inflation.

"Granted the important place of moral thought and values for economics, how should we...become aware of all the insights we have missed because of our previous, exclusive concentrations on self-interest?" Hirschman suggests that economists study altruism. Economists need to incorporate into their analysis...such basic traits and emotions as the desire for power and for sacrifice, fear of boredom, commitment, unpredictability and so on." He concedes "when one has been groomed as a 'scientist,' it takes a great deal of wrestling with oneself before one will admit that moral considerations...can effectively interfere with...impersonal forces of supply and demand."

Once social scientists "have become fully aware of our intellectual tradition with its deep split between head and heart...the first step toward overcoming that tradition and toward healing that split has already been taken." It is then possible to visualize a kind of social science that would be very efficient from the one most of us have been practicing: a moral social science where moral considerations are not repressed, but are systematically commingled with analytical argument..."

RICHARD A. MUSGRAVE–1981

Selection Committee: Kenneth J. Arrow, Arthur M. Burns,
Martin S. Feldstein,
Egon N. Neuberger, Frank W. Schiff

Fiscal Functions: Order and Politics

Pointing to a thesis first presented in his pathbreaking book *The Theory of Public Finance* (McGraw-Hill, 1959), Musgrave called for a review of budget policy which "evokes multiple goals, including provision for social goods, adjustment in income distribution and stability with growth."

Regarding provision for social goods, Musgrave maintained that a political process is needed, one based on consumer tastes, demography, technology and income level; but not set by political ideology. Involved is a "mechanism (a voting system) by which individual preference for social goods come to be revealed and payments are made to defray the costs." The voting rule and definition of issues are problems. For the first, Musgrave opts for simple majority rule. Regarding the issues, he recommends that tax and expenditure decisions be made jointly "so that (as per Knut Wicksell) voters can decide whether any particular project is worth the tax price they are asked to pay." Because different population groups value various programs differently, each group would pay different types and amounts of taxes.

Acknowledging that these suggestions run counter to popular budget procedures, he nevertheless also maintains that, though the equity rule is a mainstay of public finance, it does not address the need for linkage between both revenue-setting and expenditures based on benefits received by consumers. This process also calls into play the need for a balanced budget, with the expressed caveat that government borrowing is acceptable where capital goods are involved thus permitting "future beneficiaries to share in the cost."

While falling short of a workable solution, Musgrave's suggestions "at least point in the direction of constructive budget reform."

A major consideration in this discussion, however, is burden distribution which "may prove regressive, proportional or progressive depending on the price-and income-elasticity of demand for public services." Regardless "the benefit tax reflects the prevailing state of distribution and may thus be viewed as distributionally neutral." Furthermore, this approach could allow for tax-transfer measures "designed to adjust the prevailing state of distribution."

His second concern of fiscal policy is the state of income distribution. From the philosophy of John Locke, that one is entitled to the fruits of one's labor without state interference, to the arguments of John Rawls, that the accident of birth, with its attendant differences in talent, wealth, and position do not "establish a legitimate claim of desert," there are strong arguments regarding distributive justice. Musgrave suggests that, "The degree of redistribution which a society chooses to undertake at a given time is conditional by prevailing distribution of income and the average income level. But distribution policy also reflects social attitudes and the balance of political power." In recent decades those attitudes and political power have been responsible for growth of the public sector into the welfare state, which Musgrave believes could be a self-terminating process based on change of balance between the payors and receivors.

Another consideration in redistribution is its implementation, the most attractive method of which, in the long run, Musgrave contends, is through labor-market and training policies "aimed at raising earning power of the poor." More directly, he suggests a tax-transfer scheme; however, if such a scheme could not be achieved politically, leveling of income "could be achieved via progressive financing of an expanded provision for social goods." Taking into consideration fundamental changes in the balance between reduction of public services and reduced progressive taxation, a more efficient conduct of fiscal affairs could be realized.

With further regard to a tax transfer, Musgrave asks, "How can one explain that much of fiscal redistribution...has been through services in-kind? He suggests, "In large degree, this prevalence of in-kind redistribution reflects the desire of payors to determine how the funds should be spent by payees." In-kind transfers in general present complex problems in terms of payor or payee preferences, their financing, and what kind of goods they are, to which Musgrave claims no ready solutions.

He then considers fiscal policy as related to employment, inflation and growth. Musgrave contended that a desirable public policy would avoid such biases as are rooted in Keynesian theory. He questioned the use of increased spending to increase employment and reduced spending to reduce demand. The responsibility to "expand or restrain aggregate demand should be borne evenly by both the public and private sector and not place a disproportionate share on the former."

He calls for a "third set of adjustments" in his theme of "multiple policy instruments," a tax or transfer "which would lower or raise private income in proportional fashion, while being neutral with regard to both the provision for social goods and the distribution of income." Musgrave associates these devices with the need of a stabilization policy founded on the role of the budget. How stabilization methods are introduced, however, can affect many economic reactions, not the least of which is their influence on inflation.

He also discusses "supply-side economics." Though he questions its short-run benefits to stabilization, he accepts its longer-run influence on economic growth.

The role of taxes is of great importance on economic incentives. Their effect on various actors in the economy depends on their relationship to incentives and how taxes themselves are defined.

In consideration of the need for an orderly approach to fiscal policy, both the private and public sections play vital roles, "...I would...suggest that this dualism adds to the richness of social intercourse in a democratic society."

JANOS KORNAI–1982

Selection Committee: Kenneth J. Arrow, Arthur M. Bayer, Alan Brown, Albert O. Hirschman, Frank W. Schiff

The Health of Nations: Reflections on the Analogy Between the Medical Sciences and Economics

As an economist, Kornai asks the question, "What can we learn from another discipline?" He chooses to compare economics with medical science. Acknowledging that there are great differences between the perceptible successes and failures in each, he points out another difference: medical science can test most of its hypotheses, economics cannot.

He limits his consideration to present "diseases of the medium–and highly-developed countries" and lists seven main groups of economic diseases they are confronting. (1) Inflation, slow-creeping, galloping or, in its most fatal form, "ever-accelerating, rushing, hyper-inflation," (2) unemployment, present in a mild form in every system, but in its graver forms, "undoubtedly...a disease," (3) shortage, in which the buyer, not getting the desired commodities or services, is forced to substitute or to delay the purchase, (4) excessive growth of foreign trade, in which a country suffers from inadequate use of credits and a drifting into indebtedness, (5) growth disturbances which include many diseases such as abnormally slow growth, stagnation, or even declines in production and consumption or combinations thereof. (6) inequitable distributions, where "necessary, healthy inequality ends and where degeneration into inequality starts...(the) type that hurts the sense of justice," (7) bureaucratization, in which "distributive decisions pass from...the directly affected...into the scope of the impersonal authority" of the bureaucracy.

Kornai avers that none of the medium and highly developed countries would be completely free of each of the seven diseases and that a country would be relatively favorable "if it is tormented only by a single main disease" with two or three others in a milder form.

Defining health in economic systems presents many problems. In medicine, a definition of health is based on the premise that there are healthy people whose every organ is healthy. In economics, there is not a parallel premise. "Since history has to this very day not created an economy that is healthy in every respect, for our discipline, 'health' is merely a hypothetical category...The picture of a completely healthy economy can only be drawn in the framework of normative theory."

But Kornai does not rely upon theory. He says processes can be considered to be diseases of the economic system if (1) they cause...suffering to many members of the system, (2) "they can be shown not to appear in some economic system of the present."

In studying medicine, students "learn at least as much ...about sick organisms as about healthy ones." However, in economics, most of the data is devoted to the workings of healthy economics, very little to economic illnesses.

In the treatment of a human disease, whether therapeutic or surgical, the practitioner is concerned with after-effects of the treatment. They have to be balanced against the effects of the disease in determining what action to take. Much emphasis is placed on this reaction-factor with many volumes devoted to (1) adverse reaction patterns, (2) organs and systems, (3) risk situations, (4) interaction. Kornai wonders, "How far we (economists) are from having systematically collected the adverse side-effects of therapies!"

He then considers the seven main diseases of the current medium- and highly-developed economies and discusses the therapeutic treatment suggested by economists.

(1) Inflation. If it is treated by demand-restriction, the typical side-effects are declining production and increasing unemployment. If wage-price controls are imposed, the side-effects are disturbances in the market process and growing bureaucracy. Shortages also can be expected. "In a capitalist economy, repressed inflation takes the place of open inflation."

(2) Unemployment. In capitalist economies, if Keynesian measures are used to fight unemployment, inflation is accelerated. In socialist economies where unemployment can be eliminated by various state-imposed mechanisms, those processes are followed by the side-effects of chronic shortages, more bureaucratization, and in many cases, increases in foreign indebtedness.

(3) Shortage. To fight shortages, some controlled economies have given greater latitude to market and price mechanisms. The side effects: black markets, queueing, accelerating inflation, relative unemployment, excessive foreign indebtedness.

(4) Excessive growth of foreign indebtedness. It is treated by currency devaluation, protectionist policies, import-restrictions, export subsidies, etc. Side-effects: growth slow-down, growing unemployment in capitalist economies or domestic shortages in Eastern Europe, the usual acceleration of inflation, and further bureaucratization.

(5) Growth disturbances. In capitalistic countries, in treating cyclical fluctuations, the therapy is linked to treating unemployment. The most important side-effect is speeding up of inflation.

(6) Inequitable distribution. In the capitalist world, many countries, to fight this disease, imposed heavy and progressive taxation with free or almost free services and insurance. Progress was made but not without serious side-effects: more bureaucracy, shortages in some services, heavier burdens on state budgets, increased inflation, a weakening of work incentives.

(7) Bureaucratization. Main therapy is deregulation. Side-effects with similarities in capitalist and East-European countries: increasing inequalities in income and wealth, removal of lid on repressed inflation.

Kornai highlights this portion of his paper with this proposition: "In the course of history, whenever an advanced stage of some main economic disease came to prevail in an economic system, and a radical therapy was started, at least one other main disease developed to a conspicuous extent." He does not suggest that radical treatment should never be undertaken. He does urge economists to share with society what the side-effects may be. As in the medical treatment of a patient, the economic patient may be willing to accept the side-effects or may opt for suffering with the old problem. In any event, the cooperation and understanding of both the medical and the economic patient are essential.

Referring to the earlier discussion on risk situation and inter-action, Kornai maintains that many economists do not give con-sideration to the "concrete situation" of the patient. "They bravely propose their cherished recipes, without weighing care-fully what the particular situation of the economy in question is and how it is economically, socially and politically endan-gered." This raises additional questions on the nature of the economic diseases: are they "congenital," temporary, acute, chronic? What is the true significance of the symptoms? Kornai suggests economists tend to ignore these questions resulting in biased and distorted pictures of the problems.

Kornai concludes by referring to his suspicion of and aver-sion to most normative theories in economies in part because they try to outline "the ideal economic system or its individual parts." In medical science, its practitioners recognize the hu-man body as it is, for what it is. Economic practitioners, on the other hand, deal in what they would like conditions to be or what they should be, though there are some "who (have) the courage to state that there exist insoluble dilemmas."

Medicine, says Kornai, understands that the vast majority of people will sometimes be ill, but this does not deter medical scientists from continuing their research. Economists, on the other hand, have too much faith in rational man, the perfect market, perfect planning or an optimal social system. He urges that "the state of the world economy, and of our own discipline, should at least prompt us to exhibit due modesty to refrain from the cocksureness of the fanatical quacks, and to sincerely con-fess to the limits of our knowledge."

ROBERT M. SOLOW–1983

Selection Committee: Arthur Bayer, Alan Brown,
Zvi Griliches, Albert O. Hirschman,
Albert T. Sommers

Fiscal and Monetary Policy– Coordination or Conflict?

Fiscal policy and monetary policy "really are the only instruments we have for managing our economy as a whole." Why, then, are those responsible for this system–Congress, the Federal Reserve and the Executive Branch–so often in disagreement in pursuing a consistent and coordinated strategy?

In the face of much controversy on policy issues, Solow believes there would be general agreement by economists on his views on the conduct of monetary and fiscal policy. "The policy decisions of the Federal government do not completely determine the actual expenditure and revenue outcome in any fiscal year." Congressional votes and presidental signatures are responsible for some expenditures. But others are dependent on economic conditions. Furthermore, the revenue collections depend on "all sorts of imperfectly foreseeable and partially understood events..."

Indicators based on recorded outlays and revenues miss the mark on revealing the direction and size of fiscal policy actions. "We do need an indicator of the autonomous thrust of fiscal policy." Too simplistic are the widely accepted causes of expansionary or contractionary fiscal policy, those based on changing net demand for goods and services. Equally valid conclusions can apply on the tax side. "The routine is to estimate what the expediture and revenue totals would be if the economy were at some 'normal' standard of prosperity (the 'standard budget surplus or deficit'). When the standard deficit rises, fiscal policy has moved in the expansionary direction; when it falls, (it) has become more contractionary."

Solow then turned to monetary policy. He discussed federal deficit, how it can be financed by the Treasury or by the alternative of selling bonds to the Federal Reserve Bank. He also discussed the role of the Fed in buying bonds in the open market with base money to monetize already existing debt. By its open market transactions, the Fed's actions also influence interest rates up or down. Such "induced changes in the interest rates (are) the main link between monetary policy and the real economy of goods and services, production and income." There is another school of thought which believes that "an excess supply of money may induce purchases of a wide range of goods and services..."

There are two qualifications regarding interest rates. One, they will be affected by influences other than the actions of the Fed. Two, though you can tell the difference between expansionary and contractionary and the various degrees involved, "we have not defined a zero, a perfectly neutral monetary policy."

As for the further relationship of expansion–contraction to interest rates, the state of the economy and its anticipated direction are vital factors.

Solow then asked why it is desirable that fiscal and monetary policy be coordinated. The answer: because "fiscal policy and monetary policy can offset or reinforce one another, depending on whether they are pushing in the same direction or opposite directions." Without coordination, even if Congress, the Fed and the President react in the same direction independently, the results can be unbalancing."...non-cooperation is foolish. If analysis and goals have to be compromised, that should be done explicitly in the interest of coordinated stimulus or coordinated constraint, not by some accidental process." There are other factors at play that add to the complexity of arriving at policy, nevertheless the best interests of the country lie in fiscal and monetary policy working together.

Solow added another consideration. "There is (in 1983) wide-spread agreement that the U.S. needs a long up-swing because it has a long way to go to achieve a state of prosperity worthy of the name." In the face of high interest rates, the chances of a real recovery based on capital investment is not realistic. Add to that an escalating budget deficit and projections that standard-employment deficit is not shrinking and the picture darkens. The normally acceptable practices of fiscal expansion, monetization of the future deficit or other dips into monetary policy would not be helpful and might even prove to be self-destructive.

Solow referred to the Ronald Reagan administration's proposal wherein Congress "would commit itself now to a policy of fiscal austerity in the future, when the recovery (if there is one) will have matured." The big obstacle here is the inability of Congress to commit future Congresses not to mention the plan's general un-acceptability to many members of Congress. Nevertheless, Solow considered the idea seriously because "it points to the importance of intelligent coordination of fiscal and monetary policy." What is important in the long run, even in the face of the complexities facing its realization, is the ability to implement an effective mechanism combining fiscal and monetary stimulation–and knowing we can do it. Certainly nothing in past history indicates that such coordination has existed. Why we fail in this respect produces interesting conjectures. "Conventional wisdom says that expansion is almost always politically popular and restriction is not...The consequence is that governments tend to over-expand, to run the economy too close to the edge where the real expansion tips over into inflation. The response is inflationary. Central banks, on the other hand have a deflationary bias probably because "they see themselves as guardians of the integrity of the currency against the instructive inflationism of democracies and kings." But that's not the whole story. A consideration of the institutional structure in which monetary and fiscal policy is determined will be helpful.

The Fed, though it is responsible to Congress and could be altered by legislation, nevertheless, enjoys a reasonable degree of independence and can act quickly and flexibly certainly relative to the speed with which Congress acts on monetary policy. Fiscal policy is made by Congress and the President. Congress takes much time to act in most circumstances. The President could act quickly, but must use great skill politically as well as pragmatically. On balance, then, in fiscal and monetary matters, the Fed will usually "have the last word." However, when such policy moves in an uncoordinated way, the Congress does and should prevail. But there are problems here: (1) Congress is "too ponderous and too inexpert a body to assume direct operational control over monetary policy, (2) because governments may be overexpansionary and therefore inflationary, "a system of dual control might have its uses," (3) "I can see positive advantages in having several independent voices heard in the formulation and discussion of macroeconomic policy."

To achieve this goal of joint responsibility for fiscal and monetary policy, Solow suggests (1) the continuation of the President's annual projection of GNP with the continuing counsel of the Congressional Budget Office. (2) Suppose the FED, as a target, would also officially state to Congress and the country that it believes GNP should be commensurate with its projected monetary policy. Assuming all parties would see the value of candid projections, the aim for the same GNP targets would take us "well on the way to the mutual adoption of fiscal and monetary policy...compatible with the agreed path for the economy." There may be some technical qualifications involved and some intrinsic disagreements, not the least of which is the adoption of a common analytical foundation on which to base a policy, without which "there would be no point in looking for agreement and coordination. The important point is: the function of an explicit GNP target is to provide a focus for the coordinated fiscal and monetary policy, precisely so that monetary policy does not have to attempt an impossible task alone."

JAMES M. BUCHANAN–1984

Selection Committee: Arthur Bayer, David A. Martin, Zvi Griliches, Richard A. Musgrave, Herbert Stein

The Deficit and American Democracy

The major current economic problem is our apparent inability to improve the budgetary deficit of the U.S.A. Buchanan raised three questions: "(1) Why is American democracy apparently unable to behave in accord with the precepts of fiscal responsibility? (2) Why is this failure apparently unique to the historical experience since World War II, and, notably, to the period since the 1960s? (3) Why can economists contribute so little to the discussion?"

His answer to the first question: "politicians like to spend and do not like to tax." To the second, he argues Keynesian advocacy undermined the moral constraints which "inhibit massive resort to debt financing for ordinary governmental outlay." To the third question, Buchanan assert that "many economists are stifled in argument because they have got their analysis of public debt wrong." He adds that his views on these matters will be "much closer to those held by the general public than...among my economist peers."

Buchanan reminded us of our benefits from some federal spending and that we are likely to support that Congressman who supports that spending. Meantime, our elected officials respond to our demands. To finance these constituency demands, those elected to office can raise taxes, but there is a limit there. None of us enjoys paying taxes and certainly not increasing taxes. If necessary revenues were solely dependent upon taxation, there would be a point where taxpayers would revolt and some equilibrium would be reached.

However, to meet the needs of increasing spending without "overdoing" the taxing process, two other ways of financing spending programs are available: national governments can create money resulting in inflation which has been frequently used as a governmental financing device, yet, Buchanan noted, in the 1980's, there has been less tendency to resort to such a device. Another way of raising revenues is governmental borrowing, an action in which the government sells securities, using the money to meet its bills. Such action would appear to be a win-win situation for politicians. The voters support program expansion with no new taxes to support it.

A logical question is, if debt-issue financing is such a good idea, why isn't it used whenever funds are needed? The answer: government debts, like all debts, have to be paid and there are also "political thresholds or limits that constrain governmental borrowing." Though limited, borrowing will continue resulting in (1) larger governmental spending, (2) lower tax rates, (3) there will be some equilibrium but it will shift over time because of interest charges on the debt, those charges increasing by compounding with the ultimate result that "interest charges will exceed the size of the debt itself."

Buchanan then addresses the question, "Why do we now apparently live in what seems to be an historically new regime of deficit financing? Why did the change in the practice of fiscal politics occur only from the 1960's onwards?" To the first question, he says "...the Keynesian rationalization of deficit-financing gave politicians the opportunity to revert to their natural proclivities, that there existed no institutional rules to inhibit such revision." As for the timing of the phenomenon, Buchanan attributes it to the time-lag between the preachments of the Keynesian economists and the acceptance of the idea of deficit-financing by the policy-makers, and finally to the inability of politicians to recognize the two-sidedness of Keynesian economics.

Buchanan answers this third question concerning the "minimal contributions that modern economists seem to be making in the ongoing dialogue on the deficit..." First, "the simple welfare economics of the deficit...One of the difficulties is the economists' position on the deficit (and) the absence of an economic argument for its elimination, at least an argument that can be brought within the economists' familiar efficiency framework. The argument for fiscal responsibility must be, at base, a moral argument, and economists find themselves at a loss for words when they confront moral issues." Second, the simple economics of public debt."...Many modern economists do not know what they are confronting when they look at the deficit. They are placed in an intellectually-analytical straitjacket by their own methodology in macroeconomics."

Buchanan laments his relative lack of success in clarifying issues involved in the theory of public debt. While non-economists understand the implications of public borrowing, economists become confused "because they do not think in terms of the opportunity costs that individuals confront...correct opportunity cost reckoning suggests that the costs of the spending program that is debt financed must be borne by those persons who will be taxed in future periods..." The first step economists should take to be able to make a better contribution to deficit discussion is to "accept the elementary principles of debt issue. In order to examine the deficit as a moral issue, the intertemporal transfer that it represents must be recognized for what it is."

Regarding the prospects for fiscal reform, Buchanan stipulates two stages: "The simple economics of public debt must be understood along with the simple principles of fiscal politics." Emphasis must be placed on the immoral elements of deficit spending. To replace "the pre-Keynesian moral constraint, we can, at best, resort to explicit constitutional restrictions on political agents...closing off access to the government borrowing options."

He is not "overly optimistic that we can reform our fiscal politics," but progress has been made. "The dialogue on the 'constitutional economics' of the deficit has just begun."

GARY S. BECKER–1985
Selection Committee: Arthur Bayer, David A. Martin, Albert T. Sommers, Richard A. Musgrave, Herbert Stein

Special interests and Public Policies

Becker begins by referring to Adam Smith and his argument on the "selfish person who intends only his own gain and he is in this as in many other cases led by an invisible hand to promote an end which was no part of his intention" (*The Wealth of Nations*). A vital root to the study of economics since it was first written, it is acknowledged to apply to competition, pricing, distribution and to their relationship to firms, workers and consumers.

Becker suggests "one prominent condition (to Smith's thesis) is the absence of direct interactions between people or between firms and people (as, for example, in cases of industrial pollution). Another condition is that transactions must be feasible...Smith's conclusion does not follow when there are direct interactions or large transaction costs, and selfish behavior may not promote the general welfare."

In the political sector, though "economists usually assumed that governments are benevolent...our founding fathers knew that governments can be oppressive and that (they) cater to special interests." Their realism is reflected in our constitution. Modern economists are also becoming more realistic and are considering how governments actually behave. Because the people involved in government are selfish, there is a great tendency to extend that selfishness to governmental activity," which is influenced finally by "selfish groups with special interests."

As in other facets of private and public life, there is competition amongst pressure groups. Very often, well-organized, small groups have disproportionate influence amongst voters and legislators as a result of their frequent use of propaganda and misleading claims. Voters are especially vulnerable to pressure groups because of superficial influences such as "honest faces, political rhetoric, idealogies."

The effectiveness of pressure groups depends heavily on financial support. Though such support is often hard to obtain, successful groups are able to capture it by controlled subsidies–union dues, for example, which in turn result in the involvement of "free-riders" who would otherwise not actively support a group. The power of pressure groups may be limited by "countervailing power," the result of the formation of other groups objecting to the original groups' successes. In the case of an established subsidy, opposition to it grows over time because "the social cost of the subsidy grows over time...Therefore, the recent deregulation of airlines, banks and securities firms, and the pressure to lower income tax rates, as in flat-tax proposals, supports the implication of our analysis that political opposition to a subsidy becomes more effective when the social loss from the subsidy becomes larger."

Becker discusses industrial policy and the potential growth of the movement toward such a policy as another expression of workers, management, and other pressure groups to promote their own special interests. He asserts that "an industrial policy delays rather than hastens an economy's adjustment to adversity and changing conditions."

The power of special interests is clearly seen also in the evolution of President Reagan's proposal for tax reform." At its inception it took little account of the special interest political power, but before it went to Congress, it included some important nods to some powerful interests. Becker suggested that Congress would also inject its special interest changes before the bill became law.

Becker concludes by acknowledging the need for special interest groups even in the face of his negative evaluation. Because our political system does not guarantee the best possible approach to our problems, such groups are useful in steering governmental action to acceptable paths. Beyond that, the competition amongst pressure groups helps to assure "the implementation of desirable policies because favorably affected groups gain more from policies that raise aggregate wealth than other groups lose. Therefore, the groups benefited would spend more resources to lobby for these policies than groups harmed would spend to lobby against them." On balance, however, Becker maintains that "special interest groups are more likely...to produce unwise government policies when there is highly unequal access to political influence."

AMARTYA SEN–1986
Selection Committee: Lawrence A. Klein, David A. Martin,
Paul Craig Roberts, Robert M. Solow,
Albert T. Sommers

Welfare Economics and The Real World

The plight of welfare economics since its recent emergence has been a rocky one. Sen discussed its ups and downs in its earlier years and added, "The young subject seemed effectively dead..." But the diagnosis was premature.

The revival started with the return of utilitarian welfare economics, followed by works on such matters as income distribution and equity, fairness and justice, liberty and rights. "Traditional welfare economic analysis (including normative public finance) became the large subject that Pigou (*Wealth and Welfare* [1912]) had hoped it might become." Sen also notes that "the new discipline of social choice theory grew even faster." He then asks why welfare economics lost ground in the thirties through the fifties, what where the questions and answers involved in its decline and, finally, what are the new questions since its revival.

Sen suggests, "The approach to welfare economics that can legitimately be called 'traditional,' is undoubtedly that of utilitarianism." It relies on three elements: (1) welfarism, (2) sum-ranking, (3) consequentialism. The exact roles of these elements were not "critically examined in the controversies that led to the 'fall' of utilitarian economics..." The chief argument against it was not its informational adequacy, it was the "factual availability of that information which was denied." With further regard to these components, he adds, "the absence of interpersonally comparable utility formation would rule out sumranking in particular." The elimination of that element laid the way for the "emergence of Paretian welfare economics"...The central result...is the so-called 'fundamental theorem of welfare economics' showing a two way congruence between competitive equilibrium and Pareto optimal states..." (In making this assertion, Sen refers to the works of Arrow, Debreu, Hicks, Lange, Lerner, Samuelson).

Pareto optimality must be questioned because a "Pareto-optimal state can...be a den of inequity and wretchedness. If that condition is to be treated as *sufficient* for over-all optimality, then welfare economics must be seen to be oddly insensitive." Sen discusses other Pareto caveats which could further undermine the legitimacy of that principle as applied to welfare economics.

He then turns to compensation, consistency and information and their relationship to the Pareto principle. Compensation tests have been used in making judgements on social welfare. However, though first proposed by Kaldor (1939), their efficacy was debated by Hicks, Scitovsky, Baumol and others. The idea of compensation could be made more formidable if payment was actually made instead of using it as a "hypothetical possibility," but its effect on the Pareto principle is still questionable.

"A different line of extending the Paretian approach involved the use of the notion of a social welfare function...(which) can be seen as a systematic and consistent way of assigning values to alternative social states." It is this Bergson-Samuelson approach which addressed "the issue of what is valuable and how that might be reflected in the evaluation of different social states." It was Arrow, however, who demonstrated that "making such a social welfare function depend on individual utility orderings...and demanding that the relationship should satisfy certain elementary and commonly articulated background requirements would generate an impossibility."

Others have explored various ways of avoiding the impossibility result; Sen opted for dealing only with the informational question discussed earlier. Arrow's conditions allow only the use of utility information and only in a very limited form. His theorem "can be generalized to cover cases of *cardinal* utilities as well (See Sen, 1970), so that ordinality is not crucial to the impossibility result, but the absence of interpersonal comparability *is*, and so is the neglect of non-utility information...Indeed, all the Arrow conditions are quite standard for the utilitarian approach, and the difference between possibility and impossibility arises from the fact that interpersonal comparability of utility... is not usable in the Arrow framework."

Another form of "informational enrichment" would judge states of affairs by using non-utility information. By so doing... "social welfare judgements can be made to depend on them without running into Arrow's impossibility result." Recent social choice literature has investigated many of these possibilities, but they are ultimately based on Arrow's work"...Attention being paid to the informational question enriches the welfare-economic tradition in a way that has positive implications going far beyond merely seeking escape from Arrow's impossibility result. Arrow's pioneering work played a crucial dialectic role in all of this. The major cause of the 'fall' was, thus, also the main influence on the subsequent 'rise'."

Sen says there are two different problems in adopting welfarism. "First, social welfare need not...be a function only of individual achievements of well-being, and ...the fulfillment or violation of rights, liberties, freedoms, etc., may be taken to be intrinsically important. Second, well-being of persons need not be identified with their respective utilities. The latter is perhaps a harder issue..." Sen uses as an example of this the relative degree of pleasure an extremely deprived person receives from small mercies and, indeed, has trained himself to expect very little in terms of pleasure. The same applies in considering other forms of deprivation.

Though there is much information readily available in theoretical welfare economics, there is far more to be considered and much that is more difficult to obtain. It is the welfare economists who, by recognizing this informational lack and by making greater demands, can fill the informational gap.

WILLIAM J. BAUMOL–1981
Selection Committee: Lawrence A. Klein, Joseph A. Pechman,
G. Randolph Rice, Paul Craig Roberts,
Robert M. Solow

Regulation, Litigation, and Misdirection of Entrepreneurship

"When some of the most promising avenues for pursuit of profit, power and prestige either contribute little to the public's well-being or even threaten to damage welfare severely, one can expect with a considerable degree of confidence that *some* entrepreneurs will nevertheless be willing and even anxious to undertake them."

Baumol amplifies this point by adding that "productive entrepreneurship" should be free of policy interference while opportunities for "unproductive or destructive entrepreneurial action" should be foreclosed.

He also argues that, though he readily accepts the traditional definitions of entrepreneurs, there is more to the subject, all of which "does profoundly modify our views about policy related to entrepreneurship."

Throughout history the demonstrations of entreprenueurship have varied greatly and the aims of its practitioners have not been only money but also power and prestige. Accepting that description, then, the "robber barons" of the earlier years and the mob-chiefs of the past and present are undeniably enterpreneurs, though not in the prototypical sense nor in the mode in which Baumol's interest lies.

One of his concerns is a legal entrepreneurship which is "effectively destructive of the economy's output and wealth." As an example he refers to the "bad old days of regulation" when the Interstate Commerce Commission "was determined not to allow such minor considerations as relative inefficiency to determine which enterprises would survive in a given market." To assure the existence of even the most inefficient enterprises, the Commission governed its constituency by regulating prices, the net result being a non-competitive climate. The greater result was not innovativeness in business; success often went to "the one who provided the most innovative and effective means to co-opt the protective proclivities of the regulatory agency."

Baumol then addresses social responsibility in business decisions. Referring to Adam Smith and his "invisible hand" concept, Baumol wonders about the inconsistences abounding in today's business seeking profits and also its altruistic efforts to be of public service. In the final analysis, "Business does and should perform well in terms of the public interest where the rules of the game decree that substantial profits will be earned when and only when that firm's activities promote that interest."

Discussing the role of regulation and litigation, Baumol expresses great respect for lawyers and their role in protecting our civil liberties. But, "this is surely no justification for assumption of control over industrial activities by the nations attorneys..." Furthermore, the emphasis on legal action because of over-regulation has the net result of detracting executive attention from the running of a business to the running of a courtroom procedure and all it entails. Over-regulation "forces firms to continue in unprofitable lines of activity...in which demands demonstrate themselves to be insufficient to justify the costs that the supply of the products in question entails." Beyond this, regulation also impedes and postpones the entry of new technology because of delays in the regulatory process and by "virtually precluding any financial reward for risk and outlay of effort..."

On the other hand, though new opportunities are discouraged for efficient producers by regulation, unproductive entrepreneurs are given new opportunities "to employ ingenuity and innovation in the erection of impediments to the competitiveness of their rivals." Oftimes this takes the form of accusations of "unfair competition, predatory or destructive" action.

Many regulators and judges recognize the litigative acts of the unproductive entrepreneurs for what they are, but before claims can be rejected, the profitability of an innovation may have been irreparably injured.

As for what can be done, Baumol suggests that rules can be changed. He describes the procedure in Japan which discourages litigiousness. There, before a company can sue another on anti-trust grounds, permission must be gotten from the Japanese Trade Commission; permission is rarely given. In Europe, though there is much litigation, an "unsuccessful plaintiff is expected to bear the legal costs incurred by the defendant."

The Japanese and European approaches to this type of litigation are possible solutions for the United States. But other measures that can be taken to help redirect entrepreneurs include deregulation and "decoupling" which reduces the compensation a victim receives. This could serve "to discourage frivolous suits undertaken as fishing expeditions."

Whatever is done, Baumol says, "We must not...dismantle the protection to the general welfare offered by the anti-trust laws. However, one can hope that exercise of judgement will ensure progress on the one front without retreat on the other."

ROBERT TRIFFIN–1988
Selection Committee: James Buchanan, Irving Kristol, G. Randolph Rice, Robert M. Solow, James Tobin

The Intermixture of Politics and Economics in The World Monetary Scandal: Diagnosis and Prescription

While the Nobel Prize in Economics has been awarded to pure economic theoreticians, the Seidman Award has been given to political economists whose work represents a cross-fertilization of economics with other social sciences. This major objective of the Seidman Award sets the "controversial tone and contents of my (Triffin's) acceptance speech."

Though there was a time when "if you wish peace, prepare for war" was an acceptable stance, it has no validity now in the face of possible nuclear destruction. Yet, through the continuing efforts of the mass media to divide the world into two major opponents, the public accepts an "over-rearmament race," which continues with these consequences: 1) world wide inflation, 2) the growing threat of "preventive aggression, or of miscalculation of the other's intentions by either Russia or the U.S.

The remaining 180 countries find themselves aligned with one or another of the superpowers, seemingly with no alternative and with the knowledge that their land could receive the brunt of nuclear war.

In discussing a political prescription for this over-rearmament race, Triffin notes that mere negotiations will accomplish nothing. Each party, leaving the negotiation to the military establishment, persists in negotiating from strength. He suggests a unilateral move toward disarmament with no need for fear on the part of the initiator because each side has more nuclear weapons than are needed to destroy the other side. The argument against this proposition is that one country does not trust the other to reduce armaments. Triffin counters this by asserting every country's citizens' belief that "the danger of war comes from some other country but never from their own." He says every country has two types of minds: 1) "those who feel insecure and seek their security in making sure they are stronger than their feared opponent... 2) those who understand that their own security can best be guaranteed by the security of their conceivable opponents."

Triffin then discusses an economic diagnosis and prescription. The astronomical deficit of the United States is "the most *obvious* evidence of the need for a radical change of international economic policies and institutions..." He takes great exception to those who discount the imperative need for immediate action. The reason for the deficit and its consequences lies in the international monetary system. He foresaw the collapse of the *gold-exchange standard*, "pleaded for its replacement by a truly international monetary standard based on reserve-deposits with IMF rather than gold, dollars, and/or any *national* currencies." The gold-exchange standard, which was in a state of collapse during the 1960's and early 1970's, was replaced by a "paper-exchange standard" witnessing the continuation of the dollar as the major player in international contracts.

U.S. gross and net liabilities rose dramatically from 1980 to 1987, but the crucial difference between increases in the earlier years and the last five years of that period is that, "Up to the end of 1982, the U.S. re-exported 91% of the investments received from abroad" and only 31%, in the latter period. The rate of U.S. foreign lending showed a similar decrease in the same period. How long can it continue?

Triffin prescribes a revival of "the drive for fundamental monetary reforms on which an intellectual–if not political–consensus had been reached in 1974 by Jeremy Morse's *Committee of Twenty*," but "discarded abruptly...in the Second Amendment to the IMF Articles of Agreement." The "short-sightedness of U.S. politicians" in seeking to finance U.S. deficits "through the acceptance of the *national* U.S. currency as an *international* settlements medium "is to be expected because it reduces the need for "unpopular tax increases or reductions of expenditures." But, Triffin places the major blame on *other* countries for "being willing to extend persistently such financing to the U.S., "at a cost of unprecedented world inflation. He gives three reasons for this phenonenon: 1) the problems involved in agreeing on an alternative world currency, and the unwillingness of foreign firms to give up the benefits of an overvalued dollar(s), 2) "the disadvantages of such financing are confined primarily to a few countries with huge financing of U.S. deficits for the political advantages of U.S. contribution to their national defenses." It should be noted that the U.S. defense expenditures amounted to an international high of 6.6% of GNP in 1987.

Triffin strongly recommends the drastic reduction of U.S. defense expenditures and that such action should be spearheaded by non-military people in the disarmament negotiations now in process.

Any worldwide reforms will be dependent on U.S. participation. Meantime, other countries should 1) institute reforms and policy changes that will reduce their "overdependence on the vagaries of U.S. monetary and fiscal policies," 2) encourage U.S. participation by including in their actions means of cooperating with the U.S. on its dollar problem, and, at the same time, denying the U.S. the chance to finance its international deficits as it is currently. Triffin believes the European Community countries are "best able to take the leadership in such regional monetary agreements" because of their success in the development of the ECU concept.

Triffin then sets forth four actions as "urgent and feasible" in establishing the "ECU as a parallel currency in external transactions: 1) while no country would consider control of its national currency by foreigners, it would be willing "to negotiate appropriate controls over the issues of any joint reserve, or parallel currency..." 2) committees (headed by Giscard d'Estaing of France and Schmidt of Germany) have been established and agreements reached tentatively to promote this concept. Triffin describes possible structures of Board of Directors, surveillance groups, open-market committees which would govern a European Central Bank model. The result would be the revision of the ECU from a currency-basket to a "final reference currency vis-a-vis which every member's currency's exchange rate would itself be defined." Currency fluctuations, at first allowed to vary in a relatively narrow margin, would ultimately be reduced to zero.

Other results of his plan would include the free convertibility, at fixed rates, of member currencies; the continuing variability of exchange rates allowing for some official adjustments by one

of the governing bodies; the promotion of ECU "as the main–
or sole?–parallel currency... in the denomination and settle-
ment of international contracts and in banking and financial
transactions." The new entity would replace national currencies
and the "green" ECU in "the common agricultural policy
through the elimination of the 'monetary compensatory
amounts'."

The Bundesbank, the key player in the entire scenario, were
it to accept\the ECU as a legitimate currency, would accelerate
the ECU progress in banking and financial transactions, but
Triffin notes two qualifications to this action: 1) "full liberali-
zation of *intra-European* capital movements will most probably
require jointly concerted policies regarding speculative capital
movements between Europe and the United States, 2) even
purely intra-European capital movements may... be considered
damaging by the recipient country where it may create inflationary pressures as well as by the capital exporting country where
it may create deflationary pressures." Jointly agreed and imple-
mented controls could be helpful here. Indeed, appropriate controls over this entire monetary plan would be required to assure
its efficient operation, 3) though there is skepticism over the
proposals he advocates, Triffin points out the treaties concluded
recently in which Germany and France agree to closer coordination of monetary policy, "enabling them to accept and promote the creation of a European Central Bank," with a caveat
that the Bundesbank would, at this juncture, continue to exercise its "freedom of decision and independence..." 4) expres-
sions of strong support for "the measures leading to full
economic and monetary union of the Community have also
come from the European Parliament."

Triffin concludes his paper by observing that "the completion of the Economic and Monetary Union repeatedly promised by heads of States and Governments...are still distant and uncertain...(however) as an inveterate optimist, I hope to live long enough to see the end of this venture!"

87

Arthur M. Burns *(1981 Selection Committee)*
1978 Award Recipient
American Enterprise Institute
Washington, D.C.

Jack Carlson *(1979 Selection Committee)*
Chief Economist
United States Chamber of Commerce
Washington, D.C.

James H. Daughdrill, Jr. *(1977- Board of Trustees)*
President, Rhodes College
Memphis, Tennessee

Marvin G. DeVries *(1974 Selection Committee)*
Dean, F. E. Seidman Graduate School of Business
Grand Valley State Colleges
Grand Valley, Michigan

Martin S. Feldstein *(1980-81 Selection Committee)*
Department of Economics
Harvard University
President, National Bureau of Economic Research
Cambridge, Massachusetts

William J. Fellner *(1976 Board of Trustees)*
American Enterprise Institute
Former Member of Council of Economic Advisers
Washington, D.C.

Kurt F. Flexner *(1974- Board of Trustees;*
1974-76 Selection Committee)
Consultant to the Board of Trustees
Former Chairman, Department of Economics,
Memphis State University
Economist
Rhinebeck, New York

Richard M. Gillett *(1974- Board of Trustees)*
Chairman of the Board, Old Kent Bank and Trust
Grand Rapids, Michigan

H. Scott Gordon *(1977-78 Selection Committee)*
President, Canadian Economic Association
Indiana University and University of Toronto
Bloomington, Indiana

Kermit Gordon *(1976 Selection Committee)*
President, Brookings Institution
Washington, D.C.

R. Aaron Gordon *(1975 Board of Trustees)*
President, American Economic Association
University of California, Berkeley
Berkeley, California

Zvi Griliches *(1983-84 Selection Committee)*
Chairman, Department of Economics
Harvard University
Cambridge, Massachusetts

Walter W. Heller *(1974 Board of Trustees)*
President, American Economic Association
University of Minnesota
Former Chairman of Council of Economic Advisers
Minneapolis, Minnesota

Willie Herenton *(1987 Board of Trustees)*
President, The Economic Club of Memphis
Superintendent, The Memphis City School System
Memphis, Tennessee

Albert O. Hirschman *(1982-83 Selection Committee)*
1980 Award Recipient
School of Social Science
Institute for Advanced Study
Princeton, New Jersey

Odell Horton *(1982 Board of Trustees)*
President, Economic Club of Memphis
Judge, United State District Court
Memphis, Tennessee

Wasfy B. Iskander *(1979-80 Board of Trustees)*
Chairman, Department of Economics and Business Administration
Rhodes College
Memphis, Tennessee

Billy M. Jones *(1974-76 Board of Trustees)*
President, Memphis State University
Memphis, Tennessee

Leon H. Keyserling *(1978 Board of Trustees)*
Former Member, President's Council of Economic Advisors
Conference on Economic Progress
Washington, D.C.

Charles P. Kindelberger *(1985-86 Board of Trustees)*
President, American Economic Association
Ford International Professor of Economics Emeritus
Massachusetts Institute of Technology
Visiting Professor of Economics
Brandeis University
Lincoln Center, Massachusetts

Lawrence A. Klein *(1977 Board of Trustees;*
1986-87 Selection Committee.)
President, American Economic Association
Nobel Laureate in Economics
Professor of Economics, University of Pennsylvania
Chairman, Scientific Advisory Board, Wharton Econometrics
Philadelphia, Pennsylvania

Tjalling C. Koopmans *(1978 Board of Trustees)*
1978 President, American Economic Association
Yale University
New Haven, Connecticut

Irving Kristol *(1988-89 Selection Committee)*
Co-Editor, Public Interest Magazine
Washington, D.C.

Ira Lipman *(1985 Board of Trustees)*
President, Economic Club of Memphis
President and Chairman of the Board, Guardsmark, Inc.
Memphis, Tennessee

Paul W. McCracken *(1974 Board of Trustees)*
Edmund Ezra Day University Professor
University of Michigan
Former Chairman of Council of Economic Advisers
Ann Arbor, Michigan

Marshall E. McMahon *(1977-78 & 1984-88 Board of Trustees)*
Chairman, Department of Economics and Business Administration
Rhodes College
Memphis, Tennessee

David A. Martin *(1984-86 Selection Committee)*
International President, Omicron Delta Epsilon
Head, John Wiley Jones School of Business
College of Arts and Sciences
State University of New York
Geneseo, New York

John Meyer *(1976 Selection Committee)*
President, National Bureau of Economic Research
Cambridge, Massachusetts

Franco Modigliani *(1976 Board of Trustees)*
Nobel Laureate in Economics
1976 President, American Economic Association
Massachusetts Institute of Technology

Richard A. Musgrave *(1984-85 Selection Committee)*
1981 Award Recipient
Adjunct Professor of Economics
University of California at Santa Cruz
Santa Cruz, California

Gunner Myrdal *(1975 Selection Committee)*
1974 Award Recipient
Nobel Laureate in Economics
The Graduate Center, University of New York
New York, New York

Egon N. Neuberger *(1981 Selection Committee)*
International President, Omicron Delta Epsilon
Department of Economics
State University of New York
Stony Brook, New York

Arthur Okun *(1977 Board of Trustees)*
1979 Award Recipient
Brookings Institution
Former Member of President's Council of Economic Advisers
Washington, D.C.

Charles C. Orvis *(1981-83 Board of Trustees)*
Chairman, Department of Economics and Business Administration
Rhodes College
Memphis, Tennessee

Joseph A. Pechman *(1987 Selection Committee)*
Senior Fellow, Brookings Institution
Washington, D.C.

Charles F. Phillips, Jr. *(1979-80 Selection Committee)*
International President, Omicron Delta Epsilon
Washington and Lee University
Lexington, Virginia

Abe Plough *(1974-76 Board of Trustees)*
Chairman of the Board, Plough Incorporated
Memphis, Tennessee

Wayne Pyeatt *(1988 Board of Trustees)*
Chairman, The Economic Club of Memphis
Adjunct Professor, Special Studies
Rhodes College
Memphis, Tennessee

Eleanor Bernert Sheldon *(1976-78 Selection Committee)*
President, Social Science Research Council
New York, New York

Frederick W. Smith *(1981 Board of Trustees)*
President, Economic Club of Memphis
Chairman, Chief Executive Officer, Federal Express Corporation
Memphis, Tennessee

Ezra Solomon *(1987-88 Board of Trustees)*
Former Member, President's Council of Economic Advisers
Dean Witter Professor of Finance, Graduate School of Business,
Stanford University

Robert M. Solow *(1979-80 Board of Trustees)*
1983 Award Recipient
Nobel Laureate in Economics
President, American Economic association
Massachusetts Institute of Technology
Cambridge, Massachusetts

Albert T. Sommers *(1983, 1985-86 Selection Committee)*
Senior Vice-President and Chief Economist, The Conference Board
New York, New York

Herbert Stein *(1975 Board of Trustees; 1984-85 Selection Committee)*
1989 Award Recipient
A. Willis Robinson Professor of Economics, University of Virginia
Former Chairman of Council of Economic Advisers
Washington, D.C.

Gilbert Steiner *(1977 Selection Committee)*
President, Brookings Institution
Washington, D.C.

James Tobin *(1979-80 Board of Trustees; 1988 Selection Committee)*
Nobel Laureate in Economics
Former Member, President's Council of Economic Advisers
Yale University
New Haven, Connecticut

Marina v.N. Whitman *(1981-82 Board of Trustees)*
Former Member, President's Council of Economic Advisers
Vice President, Chief Economist, General Motors Corporation
New York, New York

Spence Wilson *(1977-78 Selection Committee)*
President, Kemmons Wilson, Inc.
Member, Board of Trustees
Rhodes College
Memphis, Tennessee

Director of Award (1977-   )

Mel G. Grinspan
Distinguished Service Professor, Emeritus
Department of Business Administration
Rhodes College
Memphis, Tennessee

Frank E. Seidman

1891–1972

After studying civil engineering at Cooper Union Institute in New York City, Frank E. Seidman earned a Bachelor of Commercial Science in 1913 and a Master's degree in 1917 from New York University. Both of these degrees were earned by attending school at night.

During this period, he served on the rate-making staff of the New York Public Service Commission, and in 1915 he became an economist for the then investment firm of Eastman-Dillon Company.

In 1917, he became a certified public accountant. He joined the firm of Seidman and Seidman in 1919; the firm had been started by his brother, M. L. Seidman, in 1910.

During World War I, he was a member of the Aircraft Production Board. This position was responsible for bringing him to Grand Rapids, Michigan, where he established residency. He later opened a branch office of the firm of Seidman and Seidman, and became a prominent civic leader of the area.

Throughout the period of World War II, he served as dollar-a-year economic advisor to the War Production Board.

His professional contributions were numerous. He and his brothers published the four-volume *Legislative History of the Federal Income and Excess Profits Taxes*. He was a co-author of a volume entitled *Financing the War* and the *Accounting Handbook*. In addition, he wrote many articles and lectured extensively on economics, accounting, business and taxation.

He served as chairman of the Citizens Advisory Committee and the Michigan Tax Study of the Michigan State Board of Accountancy.

Throughout his professional career, Frank E. Seidman was as concerned with the problems of individuals as he was with the problems of society. There were few aspects of society and man's place in it that were not of great interest to him.

Objective of the Award

The purpose of the Award is to recognize political economists who shall be defined as those economists concerned with improving the human condition by encouraging economic planning (which includes discretionary decisions in the prevention of or solution of economic problems which cannot be solved by the market). The recipient of this Award shall be selected from those economists who have attained recognized achievement by extending their public and recorded work into the domains of social, political and/or industrial inter-relationships. The Award is established with the expectation that individual and group social welfare will be advanced through cross-fertilization of the other social sciences with economic behavioral influences and values. The basis for recipient evaluation will encompass both the synthesis of existing thought in political and social economy and the path-breaking development of new concepts. The recipient of the Award is chosen by the Board of Trustees upon the recommendation of a Selection Committee composed of eminent economists with limited term of office. The Award is presented annually at a formal banquet in Memphis, Tennessee.

Criteria of the Award

The criteria stated herein are to provide guidance and direction to the Selection Committee. The recipient shall be associated with the area of political economy, as described above, and with interdependent areas of social sciences. The criteria to reflect these basic objectives of the annual Award are as follows:

1. The professional qualifications of the recipient are not restricted to any particular academic degree of specialization. The outstanding achievement both in quality and importance in the particular discipline which interrelates analytical economics with social aims whose formulation lies outside economics.

2. In making its selection, the Selection Committee and the Board of Trustees shall see that the distinguished contribution has most, but not necessarily all, of the following attributes:

    (a) It represents an actual interdisciplinary public policy approach to the work of the candidate bearing on the quality of life and which advances human welfare.

    (b) It synthesizes by innovation, change, research or teaching, and may be based on assumptions which, at the time, may not be capable of scientific proof.

    (c) It has made a significant contribution to what public policy ought to be by the societal functional interrelationship and not concerned only with its present state.

    (d) It contributes to theory and continued economic and social science analysis of the existing body of theoretical concepts.